# DOING RIGHT

# IN A

# WRONG WORLD

*Bishop Darryl S. Brister*

# DOING RIGHT
# IN A
# WRONG
# WORLD

Unless otherwise noted, all Scripture quotations are from *The New King James Version* of the Bible, copyright © 1979, 1980, 1982, by Thomas Nelson, Inc., Nashville, Tennessee. References marked "KJV" are from the Authorized King James Version of the Bible.

**DOING RIGHT IN A WRONG WORLD**

ISBN 1-880809-45-1

Printed in the United States of America

Copyright © 2005 by Darryl S. Brister

Legacy Publishers International

1301 South Clinton Street

Denver, CO  80247

Phone: 303-283-7480  FAX: 303-283-7536

Library of Congress Cataloging-in-Publication Data Pending

# Dedication

To Dr. Dionne F. Brister, my wife and co-laborer in the gospel—your growth, strength, tenacity, and faithfulness to both our family and the family of God are remarkable! To my mother who taught me to do right as a child—thank you for the proper foundation.

To my children, Darrlynn, D.J. Darielle, Trey, and Tyza—all of you are uniquely special. To the Family of Light (New Orleans, Houma, Hammond, Baton Rouge, and Haiti)—God is faithful!

Finally, I dedicate this book to every Eagle Christian who is determined to fulfill their assignment. Keep flying while fighting!

Together we have a dream and desire to raise up leaders who will make a difference in the lives of millions of people.

# Acknowledgements

I'd like to thank the many leaders who helped me while I was working on this book. I must always thank God for the men and women of God who have been and continue to be committed to my forming. To my father in ministry, Bishop Paul S. Morton; to my father in the faith, Bishop Nate Holcomb; to Pastor John C. Raphael Jr., thanks for the trip to Panama; to Pastor Keith L. Clark and Pastor Lee Fields, this book is a result of our conversations and experiences in Panama.

To Bishop Charles E. Blake, Bishop T.D. Jakes, Bishop Eddie L. Long, Bishop Neil C. Ellis, Bishop Carlton Pearson, Bishop Noel Jones, Prophet Aubrey Shines, and Pastor Melvin Wade—all of you will remember what we talked about.

I must say thank you to Harold McDougal, my managing editor at Legacy Publishing International for all his patience and assistance as we worked through the manuscript. I also want to thank my executive assistants, Samantha Merritt and Jeronda Bordenave, whose great hearts and incredible service make me a better leader.

Finally, I want to thank all of my spiritual sons and daughters, the leaders of Full Gospel, the leaders of Beacon Light International Ministries, and the staff and volunteers of both DSB Ministries and Beacon Light International Baptist Cathedral.

# Contents

*For He made Him who knew no sin to be sin for us, that we might become the righteousness of God in Him.*

2 Corinthians 5:21

# Introduction

One day some months ago the Lord said to me, "Son, the way you see things is not necessarily the way they are. It's just the way you perceive them." That let me know that it's time that we Christians get a revelation of things as God's sees them. Our perceptions are often in error, but His never are.

Our loving God wants to take us from where we currently are to where He wants us to be, but the only way that can happen is if we can somehow gain a new and different perspective on life. If we continue to see things as we have seen them in the past, we will make very little progress.

The day I saw this clearly I made up my mind to allow the Lord to change me from the inside out. What I had considered law was not necessarily His way of doing things, and I desperately wanted His ways. I would have to open myself to Him as never before and learn from His Spirit. He had said:

*"For My thoughts are not your thoughts, nor are your ways My ways," says the Lord. "For as the heavens are higher than the earth, so are My ways higher than your ways, and My thoughts than your thoughts."*

Isaiah 55:8-9

The local church, I was convinced, had been taken into areas that God had never intended, and, in the process, we had confined ourselves as individuals to a man-made image of what was expected of us. We were trying to be as "good" as possible, but in the process we were way off target.

When an airplane takes off from our local Louis Armstrong Airport here in New Orleans bound for some other city, there's an onboard navigation system that will guide the plane on its designated flight path. Pilots talk to air traffic controllers, and on the basis of the orders they receive, the navigation system is set. But if that navigation system is as much as one degree off, and the plane flies on that slightly deviated course for several hours, the plane could find itself in a totally different location. If the flight was intended for Atlanta, for example, but it flew slightly off course for several hours, it might not even be over the state of Georgia.

One degree off is a serious deviation when multiplied by hundreds of miles flown, and that's just how serious this business of proper perspective is to Christians everywhere today. The wise King Solomon spoke of the *"little foxes that spoil the vines"* (Song of Songs 2:15).

All of us have little things in our lives that are throwing us off course and causing us serious frustration. They may be so small that an observer would hardly notice them, but to our hope of achieving our ultimate destiny, they are huge. If left unchecked, these little things could wreak havoc with our spiritual lives.

Personally, I'm convinced that one of these little things that have been hindering many Christians is their desire to be "good." "Lord, make me a 'good' Christian," many fine people pray. "Make me a 'good' mother (a 'good' father, a 'good' supervisor, a 'good' business owner, a 'good' judge)." And who could find fault with such a prayer?

The problem is that "goodness" is man's measure of accomplishment. God never called us to be "good"; He called us to be "right." There's a huge difference between doing the "good" thing and doing the "right" thing. This is an important distinction.

As long as we're only doing "good," we're working in the flesh, striving for man's approval. Doing "good" can never make us righteous, and righteousness is required if we are to be part of God's kingdom. It's time that we begin concentrating on what is "right" in God's eyes.

When I began teaching a series of sermons on this subject to our people in New Orleans, it was life-changing—both for me and for them. During that time, I also began to receive direct attacks from the enemy like none I had ever experienced before. It was because our people were being freed from false concepts to serve God in liberty, and the devil didn't like that. But I kept preaching the truth, and people kept being set free. Now, for the first time, I offer those liberating teachings to a wider audience.

I'm very excited about God's Word and about what He is doing in the lives of His people today, and I challenge every reader who picks up this book: Let the Word of God set you free and put you on the path of *Doing the "Right" Thing.*

*Bishop Darryl S. Brister*
*New Orleans, Louisiana*

# CHAPTER 1

# What Does It Mean to Do the "Right" Thing?

*For He made Him who knew no sin to be sin for us, that we might become the righteousness of God in Him.*

2 Corinthians 5:21

God has called us to become *"the righteousness of God in [Christ Jesus],"* and for most of us, that's a scary thought. But it shouldn't be. Righteousness does not mean, as many have imagined, a state of absolute perfection. It simply means to be in right standing with God. It means that you've chosen the "right" path in life and that you're endeavoring to do the "right" thing in God's eyes from day to day.

## GOODNESS VS. "RIGHTNESS"

God never intended for us to become "good"; He always intended for us to become "right." There were many people in the Bible who did "good" things but failed to do the "right" thing. There's a difference. We'll look at some of them in a later chapter. But first, let's firmly establish the basis for the message of this book.

These words *good* and *right* are, in many ways, interchangeable in our thinking. *Good*, as we commonly use it, means "to be positive or desirable in nature." In light of this, most of us are pretty good, some of us are becoming good, and a few of us are already good. But are we "right"?

The word *right*, as found in the New Testament, is translated from the Greek word *geikos*, and it is sometimes also translated as *just*. When the New Testament Scriptures (quoting Habakkuk 2:4) speak of the just living by faith, this phrase *"the just"* could also be translated as *"the right"*:

*For in it [the Gospel] the righteousness of God is revealed from faith to faith; as it is written, "The just shall live by faith."*

Romans 1:17

So, *"the ['right'] shall live by faith."* What exactly is "right"? The definition of *right* is "conforming to justice." It means that we do something, not because we're fearful of the consequences of doing otherwise, but because it's the right thing to do.

So there's a definite difference between doing what's "good" and what's "right," and the objective of the enemy is to convince you and me to become comfortable with just doing what's acceptable, not what God requires of us. The enemy knows that if you can become satisfied with doing what is "good," what's acceptable in man's eyes, you'll never put forth the effort necessary to do what's "right," what pleases God. And in order for you to become the righteousness of God, you must be "right," not just "good."

There are three possible positions of righteousness. There is unrighteousness, self-righteousness, and the righteousness of God, and we all know which one we should choose. If your motivation is not to become righteous, there are certain things in life that you'll never receive. God will always command a blessing on those who are righteous. So if we've been taught only to be "good" and not to move toward righteousness, we need to relearn God's desires for our lives. God is saying that we must do what is "right." That may not be the easy thing to do, but it *is* the way of blessing.

## RIGHTEOUSNESS, OR "RIGHTNESS" IS FOUND ONLY THROUGH CHRIST

Again, to be righteous does not mean to be perfect. It means that you're in right standing with God—regardless of your past, regardless of your struggles, regardless of how many mistakes you've made, and regardless of what type of family you come from. Paul wrote to the Church:

*Therefore, if anyone is in Christ, he is a new creation.*

2 Corinthians 5:17

How does this new birth take place? It happens through the process of regeneration. God gives you a new spiritual genetic makeup and changes your DNA in the Spirit. Paul explained it further with the words I have chosen as the theme verse for this book: *"He made Him who knew no sin to be sin for us, that we might become the righteousness of God in Him"* (2 Corinthians 5:21).

So where does any righteousness that may be found in us come from? It can only come from God through Jesus Christ. There is no other source of righteousness. Any righteousness that we attempt to display ourselves outside of Christ is nothing but *"filthy rags"*:

*But we are all like an unclean thing, and all our righteousnesses are like filthy rags; we all fade as a leaf, and our iniquities, like the wind, have taken us away.*

Isaiah 64:6

True righteousness is found in Christ, and to be truly righteous is to be in Him. This doesn't mean that we will not make mistakes and fall short of the mark God has set for us. But the Scriptures teach us:

*If we confess our sins, He is faithful and just to forgive us our sins and to cleanse us from all unrighteousness.*

1 John 1:9

God's promise to cast the sins of those who come to Him into the sea of forgetfulness is not just for new believers. It's for all believers of all ages and all levels of experience.

Men are slow to forget our failures, but not God. With Him, the past is past, and He looks at us based on our status in Christ, not on the basis of our past failures. When He cleanses us from unrighteousness, He also frees us from the penalty of it. When men look at us, they see us through the filter of our fragile record, but when God looks at us, He sees us through the filter of the righteousness found in His Son. He became sin for us so that we could be freed from its power.

Without any hesitation or reservation, lay hands on yourself right now and pray, "Lord, make me righteous." He can do it, and He *will* do it.

Don't be afraid of this word *righteous*. Let go of your wrong concepts of the past, and see "rightness" and righteousness as God sees them. Christ paid the price so that you could become the righteousness of God. Start acting like His righteousness.

As Jesus hung on the cross, God, through Him, was reconciling man back to Himself, back to his original state, back to what he had enjoyed before the Fall. All that the sin of Adam and Eve had brought upon man was being dealt with once and for all. That's why, as Jesus hung there from the sixth to the ninth hours, the veil of the Temple was supernaturally parted, and a way was made into the Holy of Holies, the very presence of God.

Just as in natural birth, where there is a release of water and blood, in this spiritual rebirthing of man, water and blood were released from Jesus' side.

Jesus had not sinned, and there was no reason for Him to suffer the consequences of sin. But God allowed Him to become sin for you and me, so that we could live "right" in this world. You can never become righteous by doing "good."

God made Jesus to become sin. He had to become everything that we were so that we could become everything that He is. He is righteous, and He is calling us to righteousness.

## MAN WAS CREATED "RIGHT"

When God created Adam and Eve, He created them "right," or righteous. It was only after sin had entered into the world that they were no longer experiencing His righteousness and no longer doing what was "right." It was in that moment that man's never-ending quest for goodness began, and that quest continues today.

It was Adam who got us all into this mess, so that we needed a Savior to bring us back into our original state with God. That original state was one of right standing with Him. That state was lost through Adam, but it can be regained through Christ.

Jesus *"knew no sin,"* but God allowed Him to become sin *"for us,"* so that we could become *"the righteousness of God,"* so that we could become "right" in and through Christ Jesus. From the outset, the goal God set for His children was never that they simply become "good." It was always that they become "right." When you catch of glimpse of your right standing with God, your entire life will change.

Again, this doesn't mean that I'm perfect. It means that if and when I fall short, the Spirit of God on the inside of me will convict me of wrong, and because I have a desire to be right, I will seek restoration. When I do wrong, in order to restore my righteousness with God, I must confess my wrong, seek God's forgiveness and His help not to repeat the error. As soon as this happens, I'm restored to my place of righteousness.

If I were to ask a given congregation how many of them were "righteous," not many would raise their hands. This shows that our understanding of this word is in error. We are the righteousness of God in Christ Jesus, and He has called us to live "right" in this world.

## ALLOWING GOD TO CORRECT OUR COURSE

As Christians, many of us have given God free course to correct us in some areas of our lives and absolutely no freedom to correct us in others. We have areas that are actually off limits to His Spirit, areas that we don't allow Him to touch. This must change, for it's time to bring the entirety of our lifestyles into conformity with God's righteousness, time to let Him have His way in every area of our lives, time to become *"the righteousness of God,"* time to start doing what is "right."

Why should we want to do this? It's only when we come into conformity with God's righteousness that we can be blessed in the measure God desires. Awesome rewards await those who are willing to go God's way. So what are we waiting for? Let's allow God to make us the righteousness of God in Christ Jesus. Let's start doing the "right" thing.

The root of the word *righteousness* is, of course, the word *right*, and this word means "the quality of being right." How can we be "right" in everything? That can only happen as we are in Christ Jesus, and He is in us. Let God start the work in you today. Right now, lay hands on yourself and fervently pray this prayer: "Lord, make me righteous." Then let this be your daily prayer, not to be "good," but to be "right." And know that God can answer that prayer. He can make you His righteousness.

*When you begin to see your right standing with God, your whole life, everything about you, will change.*

You should desire to be righteous so that you can produce the fruits of righteousness and also so that you can receive the benefits of being righteous. Many of us in the Church have been "good," but relatively few of us have been "right." It's time to change all that. It's time for righteousness to prevail.

God is ready to channel His blessings, His will, His purpose, and His plan through the lives of those who are willing to become "right" and not just "good." After all, He has destined us to become *the righteousness of God in Him,* and it's time that we made progress toward that goal.

When you begin to see your right standing with God, your whole life, everything about you, will change. You'll move into a whole new area of faith, and the fruits of the Spirit will flow from your life as never before.

## WHAT THIS CHANGE MEANS

This is where the Lord has me right now, and I believe it's where He wants us all to be at this point in our spiritual development. I no longer want to be in just a "good" place; I want to be in the "right" place. If I'm just in a "good" place, there are certain things that I'll have to go after and get for myself. But if I'm in the "right" place, God will bring those things to me. Our lives in the past have been much too taxing because much of what we have attained has been attained by our own goodness, not by His righteousness working in us. But it's now a new day for those who are willing to change.

Things are not happening the way they should be happening for many of us because we've been in a "good" place, but not the "right" place. We've had "good" ideas, but we've not embraced "right" ideas. "Right" ideas have a way of challenging even our "good" ideas.

In reality, righteousness is goodness grown up, goodness matured, so if you're ready to mature in God, this blessing is for you. And many of the things that have been happening in your life have been allowed by God to mature you and bring you into righteousness.

The apostle Paul wrote:

*When I was a child, I spoke as a child, I understood as a child, I thought as a child; but when I became a man, I put away childish things.*

1 Corinthians 13:11

When you move from trying to be "good" and start becoming righteous and doing "right," your thinking will change, your speech will change, and your actions will change. So what are we waiting for? Let's get started.

## IS DOING THE "RIGHT" THING TOO HARD?

Why does it often seem too hard to do the right thing? It's because we have an enemy who is dedicated to keeping us down. If he cannot drag us down into blatant sin, then he satisfies himself by convincing us to do what is "good" rather than what is "right." And if he can accomplish this, he wins.

It's possible to have a "good" spirit and not have the "right" spirit. This is true of many well-known ministries and ministers. They have platforms, prestige, position, anointing, talents, gifts, and abilities, and yet something is missing. It's time for righteousness, time to live to please the God of heaven.

This teaching will force you into maturity if you allow it to, and many of us need that. James spoke of those who were only *"hearers"* of the Word and not *"doers"*:

*But be doers of the word, and not hearers only, deceiving yourselves.*

James 1:22

Those who are only "hearers" deceive others, but they also deceive themselves. The fact that they faithfully make an effort to hear the Word is such a "good" thing that they are thought of as also being obedient to what they hear.

But this is not necessarily so. Far too many hear, but then they never bring themselves to the point of changing their way of thinking, their way of speaking, and their way of living. In their eyes, they're already "good" enough, and therefore they have no motivation to change further.

## IT'S TIME FOR CHANGE

The reason for the phenomenon we are calling "the generation gap," the huge gulf between parents and their children, is a difference in perspective. Children can never seem to see things the way their parents do, and parents can never seem to see things the way their children do. This is because parents have had experiences that now affect the way they look at everything in life.

Parents are much more cautious, much more skeptical, and much more concerned with consequences. Children, because of their lack of experience, are not burdened by any of these things.

Young people fall in love so easily and are immediately convinced that they've found the person of their dreams. Parents can often take one look at that "dream person" and say with confidence, "This is not the right person for you." That doesn't make sense to a young lady. This individual has shown a liking for her, he's cute, and he has a car. She, therefore, is looking forward to having a date with him.

The parent, however, is looking at this young man from a different perspective. Would he make a suitable mate for life?

Young people are looking for a good date, but parents see consequences down the road. This ability to foresee consequences denotes maturity, and that's why we immediately recognize that those who do silly things, not considering the consequences of their actions, are immature.

Paul knew what it meant to grow up spiritually. He was now thinking differently, talking differently, and acting differently, and that's what maturity brings.

God is moving us into maturity, and part of that process is a dramatic change in our thinking. We need a new perspective on life, a whole new way of looking at things. It's time that we understood the difference between settling for "good" and insisting on "right."

## LOOKING FOR THE "RIGHT"

Many single people have been praying the wrong kind of prayers. They've been asking God for a "good" mate, when what they need is the "right" mate.

We often call the person they're seeking Mr. Right or Ms. Right, and that's what they need to be. A "good" man could never love a woman the way Christ loved the Church, and yet that's exactly what believers are called to do. This demands righteousness.

Don't be satisfied with a "good" job; pray until you have found the "right" job. If you're on the "right" job, your stress levels will decrease dramatically.

Stop settling for a mediocre job just because it pays well. Some people are making more money than they've ever made, but they can't enjoy it. They have no peace. The work they're doing is not what God has called them and prepared them to do. And so they're not happy doing it.

Your quest for the "good" things in life must end today, and your quest for the "right" things must begin. This will enable you to begin *Doing "Right" in a Wrong World.*

# CHAPTER 2

# God's Call to "Rightness"

*Hear, O heavens, and give ear, O earth! For the Lord has spoken: "I have nourished and brought up children, and they have rebelled against Me; the ox knows his owner and the donkey its master's crib; but Israel does not know, My people do not consider."*

Isaiah 1:2-3

Isaiah exposed the lack of "rightness" in his day, and through him God issued a call to all men everywhere to return to that standard.

This particular passage from Isaiah deals with the wickedness of the people of Judah, against whom God had a complaint. He had raised them up for one purpose, and they were doing something altogether different. They had become rebellious against their Creator.

## GOD IS TIRED OF MERE GOODNESS

Isaiah continued with some rather stark language:

*Alas, sinful nation, a people laden with iniquity, a brood of evildoers, children who are corrupters! They have forsaken the Lord, they have provoked to anger the Holy One of Israel, they have turned away backward.*

Isaiah 1:4

God was tired of "goodness" and was now demanding "rightness":

*Hear the Word of the Lord, you rulers of Sodom; give ear to the law of our God, you people of Gomorrah: "To what purpose is the multitude of your sacrifices to Me?" Says the Lord. "I have had enough of burnt offerings of rams and the fat of fed cattle. I do not delight in the blood of bulls, Or of lambs or goats."*

Isaiah 1:10-11

Surely the offerings these men had made to God were "good," but God was no longer accepting their "good" offerings. "Good" wasn't good enough. He called these offerings *"futile sacrifices":*

*"When you come to appear before Me, who has required this from your hand, To trample My courts? Bring no more futile sacrifices."*

Isaiah 1:12-13

God was no longer impressed with such offerings, for they failed to meet His specifications. And there was more of the "good" that displeased Him:

*"Incense is an abomination to Me. The New Moons, the Sabbaths, and the calling of assemblies—I cannot endure iniquity and the sacred meeting."*

Isaiah 1:13

Even prayers now offended God, and He refused to hear them:

*When you spread out your hands, I will hide My eyes from you; Even though you make many prayers, I will not hear. Your hands are full of blood.*

Isaiah 1:15

These people needed to get things "right" before God would accept them. This demanded cleansing and repentance:

*"Wash yourselves, make yourselves clean; put away the evil of your doings from before My eyes. Cease to do evil."*

Isaiah 1:16

## "LEARN TO DO GOOD"

But none of this comes easily or automatically. How can we make the changes God is demanding of us? First, we must experience a transformation in our thinking. We must *"learn to do good,"* to do things God's way:

*"Learn to do good; seek justice, reprove the oppressor; defend the fatherless, Plead for the widow."*

Isaiah 1:17

If these people wanted to be God's people, they had to get it "right." They had to learn to do well, seeking to know what was really important to God. This included seeking justice, rebuking the oppressor, defending the fatherless, and pleading for the widows. In short, these people needed a totally different perspective on life. As it was, they were walking all over people who needed them, and they didn't even care. They had to *"learn to do well."*

Isaiah went on to speak for the Lord:

*"Come now, and let us reason together," Says the Lord.*

Isaiah 1:18

These words were written to individuals who considered themselves to be the people of God. They had been doing "good" and doing it in the Lord's name, but they had not been doing what was "right" in His sight. Therefore, He told them it was time for change.

They were bringing sacrifices to the Lord, so that wasn't the issue. The issue was that they were bringing their sacrifices with the wrong spirit. Their traditions were not bad, but their hearts were. Their hearts and minds needed to be changed.

## CHANGE OR ELSE

Change was clearly available to them. God said to them:

*"Though your sins are like scarlet, they shall be as white as snow; though they are red like crimson, they shall be as wool. If you are willing and obedient, You shall eat the good of the land."*

Isaiah 1:18-19

But what if they refused to change? When we read this passage, we usually stop with these verses, but God didn't stop there. He was serious about this thing. He went on to say:

*"But if you refuse and rebel, you shall be devoured by the sword"; for the mouth of the Lord has spoken.*

Isaiah 1:20

God was setting a clear ultimatum for these people. He had had enough of their phoniness. And He had been patient and tolerant of their abuses of His house long enough. He was tired of their pride and their self-righteousness. It was time for them to do "right," to get His righteousness. And, if they were not willing to do that, it was time for them to die. That was the choice the Lord presented them with.

*People are easy to fool, but God can never be fooled.*

God was trying to send these people in a different direction, to give them a different perspective, but it was up to them to receive it or reject it. That choice meant the difference between life and death, blessing and cursing.

God was serious. This is not a game. He means business with His people.

Why do we continue to think that we can fool God? People are easy to fool, but God can never be fooled. He knows everything about us. It's time to make some hard decisions about life, and if we're not able to chose "right," the results may be tragic. God is tired of lip service and now demands that we serve Him in truth—or else.

This is as it should be. When we profess to be people of God, more is expected of us. Christians are held to a much higher standard than are the people of the world. If you're a follower of Christ, you will be called upon to do things that other people will not be required to do, and you will be forbidden to do some of the things others are permitted to do.

## WHEN GOD'S WILL IS NOT TO OUR LIKING

You may not always like the path God has chosen for you. Even Jesus faced something He felt He could not handle. It happened as He was praying in the Garden of Gethsemane the night before His death:

*He went a little farther and fell on His face, and prayed, saying, "O My Father, if it is possible, let this cup pass from Me; nevertheless, not as I will, but as You will."*

Matthew 26:39

Jesus was telling the Father that He didn't want to do this thing. Was there not some other way it could be done? Knowing the purpose for which He had come to earth, in the end, He relented and submitted Himself to the Father's will, and as followers of Christ, we must do the same.

What Jesus did in the garden to overcome His flesh and do the "right" thing can be instructional to us. First, He was brutally honest with God in prayer, and we must do the same. Tell the Lord, "I have a serious problem in this particular area, and I really need help."

You might pray, for instance, something like this: "Procrastination has been a part of me for a very long time, and it's making me miss out on too much. I need help, Lord." Or you might need to pray, "Lord, my discipline is nearly nonexistent. Help me."

Whatever your particular area of need happens to be, God is ready to help you—if you'll just be honest with Him. He's just waiting to hear your cry, and the moment you cry out to Him, He'll begin moving you into a place of righteousness.

Doing the "right" thing will not come easily, or automatically. You will have to *"learn to do well."* Also, doing the "right" thing is not always popular, and it even goes against your own flesh. The flesh is often willing to do what is "good," but rarely is it willing to do what is "right." You will have to bring your flesh into subjection if you hope to find God's perfect plan for your life.

The simple reason that so many Christians live "good" but not "right" is that they're not willing to bear the pain that doing what is "right" will surely bring them. But if Jesus gave His life so that you could be righteous, you can also bear a little pain to make it happen. (This is such an important point that Chapter 10 will expand on it further.)

There would have been no life without Christ's death. In order for us to live, He had to die. This means that there is no life without death, and no resurrection without a crucifixion. Get ready to have your flesh crucified.

But even after He had suffered death by crucifixion, Jesus rose again. That gives us hope. It means that we'll never be a failure unless we choose to quit. Failing does not make us a failure; only quitting does. If we *"learn to do well,"* we are answering God's call to "rightness." And this will help us to begin *Doing "Right" in a Wrong World.*

# CHAPTER 3

# When Doing the "Right" Thing Became Abnormal Behavior

*Behold, I was shapen in iniquity; and in sin did my mother conceive me.*

Psalm 51:5 KJV

Doing the "right" thing has never been normal for those of us who are living today. Like so many generations before us, we were born in sin and *"shapen in iniquity."* So when did the "right" thing cease to be the norm for mankind and become opposite to our nature? It was, of course, when Adam and Eve sinned in the garden.

## ADAM AND EVE "BLEW IT BIGTIME"

Adam and Eve did not just sin. As we say in the vernacular of the day, they "blew it bigtime." They "went way off the deep end." God told them exactly what to do and exactly what not to do and what the consequences would be. Still, for some reason, they disobeyed Him.

The details of this incident are important because of what we have come to call the law of first mention. This theological law implies that the details surrounding the first mention of any subject in the Bible are significant and lay a groundwork for us to understand it.

In Eden, Eve ate first from the forbidden tree, and when she saw that no apparent harm came to her as a result of it, she gave the fruit to Adam, and he ate it too. It was at this point that God appeared to them and let them know in no uncertain terms that because they had insisted on doing their own thing, they were no longer innocent in His sight. They were sinners, and they would pay the price for their sin.

*Tragically, there are many members of the body of Christ who are walking around today clothed only with fig leaves.*

When Adam and Eve next heard God's voice in the garden, they ran and hid themselves. Until then, they had looked forward to fellowship with Him. Now they were estranged from God, and they feared His presence.

They were also suddenly uncomfortable with their surroundings and decided to sew fig leaves together and make aprons to cover their shame. Since that day, man has been estranged from God and has been sewing fig leaves together to hide his shame. On that fateful day, he lost his innocence. "Right" was no longer the norm.

Tragically, there are many members of the body of Christ who are walking around today clothed only with fig leaves. *"Seek justice,"* God said. *"Learn to do good."*

## THE STRUGGLE OF ADAM'S OFFSPRING WITH DOING "RIGHT"

Not only Adam and Eve lost the innocence of Eden and the normalcy of "right." Their children and grandchildren and their children and grandchildren suffered the same fate. Cain, the son of our first forebears, committed a terrible sin in killing his brother. When he did this, God said to him, *"If you do well, will you not be accepted?"*:

*So the Lord said to Cain, "Why are you angry? And why has your countenance fallen? If you do well, will you not be accepted? And if you do not do well, sin lies at the door. And its desire is for you, but you should rule over it."*

Genesis 4:6-7

18

God's words, *"but if you do not do well,"* mean if you fail to do what's "right." That's when *"sin lies at the door."* Doing anything less than "right" is sin.

This phrase *"sin lies at the door"* means sin crouches or hides at the entrance. This language virtually personifies sin as a demon crouching like a crazed animal at Cain's doorstep, ready to pounce on him.

Is sin crouching at the door of your house? If so, before you can get out into the community, before you can get out into the workforce, before you can get out to develop some additional relationship, you have to pass through sin. Too many times, *"sin lies at the door"* because what's going on in the house may be "good," but it's not "right."

Cain was guilty of the first murder in human history:

*Now Cain talked with Abel his brother; and it came to pass, when they were in the field, that Cain rose against Abel his brother, and killed him.*

Genesis 4:8

It is ironic that the first murder recorded in the Scriptures is of a brother killing his brother. And now, thousands of years later, we still have brothers killing brothers.

The reason Cain killed his brother was that he had a problem with the way God was blessing Abel's obedience. This tragic turn of events was, no doubt, doubly tragic for Eve when she realized that she was responsible for it.

Nevertheless, God called Cain to account:

*Then the Lord said to Cain, "Where is Abel your brother?"*

Genesis 4:9

God never asks a question, expecting us to inform Him. Never think that He's waiting for our answer so that He can know what to do next. Never! God already knew the answer to His question. He just wanted to see what Cain's response would be. And his reaction was not good:

*And he said, "I don't know. Am I my brother's keeper?"*

Genesis 4:9

This uncaring attitude concerning a brother has been all too typical down through the centuries. And God wasn't pleased at all:

*And He said, "What have you done? The voice of your brother's blood cries out to Me from the ground."*

Genesis 4:10

Cain had no brotherly love, for brotherly love accepts responsibility for one another.

## BROTHERLY LOVE ACCEPTS RESPONSIBILITY

Demos Shakarian, Founder and President of the Full Gospel Business Men's Fellowship International, is quoted in the *Spirit Filled Life Bible* as saying: "The theme of brotherhood emerges early in Scripture; and from the very beginning, it is clear that God places a high priority on how brothers treat each other."[1] That includes sisters too.

Chances are that if things are not right between you and your brother (or sister), then things are not right between you and God. If things are not right between you and the people you have relationship with, chances are that things are not right in your relationship with God. God places a high priority on how we treat one another.

Dr. Shakarian continued: "In this passage, the question of responsibility for one another first emerges. Cain asks, *'Am I my brother's keeper?'* The word used for *'keeper'* (Hebrew *shamar*) means 'to guard, to protect, to attend, or to regard.' Are we responsible? 'Absolutely,' is God's answer. Not only are we our brother's keeper, we are held accountable for our treatment of and our ways of relating to our brothers (blood and spiritual)."[2]

Yes, we are expected to cover one another. Yes, we are expected to serve one another. Yes, we are expected to tend to each other's needs. That doesn't mean that we will agree on everything. We won't. But still we are to be our brother's keeper, and we will be held accountable for our treatment of our brothers. As Dr. Shakarian stated, this refers to both blood brothers and spiritual brothers.

He concluded: "For Cain's sin against his brother, God curses him throughout the Earth, takes away his ability to farm, and sentences him to a life as a fugitive and a vagabond (v. 12). This clearly indicates that unbrotherliness destines one to fruitlessness and frustration of purpose."[3]

Is this perhaps the reason that some of us cannot seem to *"eat the good of the land"* as God has promised (Ezra 9:12 and Isaiah 1:19)? Yes, if we're not doing right by our brother, what can we expect?

Abel had done nothing wrong against his brother, but Cain hated him anyway, and eventually killed him. God so took offense at that senseless act that he cursed Cain for life.

The conflict between these two brothers had its roots in the offerings each chose to give to God. Cain did bring God an offering, but Abel gave God of the firstborn of his flocks. When God accepted Abel's offering and rejected Cain's, the older brother was infuriated. He caught Abel in the field and argued with him.

"Who do you think you are?" he must have shouted. "You're my baby brother, and yet you want all the attention. Why did you think you have to give God the firstborn?" The argument escalated until Abel lay dead on the ground.

What does all of this mean to us? God is trying to move us from goodness to righteousness, to bring us into right standing with Him, and part of doing the "right" thing is knowing our responsibility toward our brothers.

## GET OVER WHAT HINDERS YOU

What is it about you that has the enemy so intimidated that he can't leave you alone? He has thrust you into one situation after another. He seems to be constantly on the attack. It's because he knows that if he can get you to deviate just one degree to one side or the other, he can make you miss the mark. Just a little give here or there will lead you somewhere God never intended you to be.

Sometimes we consider the small things in our lives that hinder us to be so "itty bitty" that they are inconsequential. We could have corrected them long ago, but didn't. We could have changed, but didn't. Now God is demanding that change for those who want to move on to greater things.

Some of us feel that we just have to win every argument and always be proven right. We always have to get in the last word, and we let people know that they'd better not "mess" with us. In the meantime, these "itty bitty" things have thrown us off course just enough that we're in danger of missing the mark. And this has caused us to experience pain that was never intended for us.

I pray that any lack of excellence will now begin to grieve you, that you will now find yourself uncomfortable around people who have words but no actions.

## THE STRUGGLE FOR RIGHT

I would not want to suggest that doing the "right" thing will always be easy. Even Paul the apostle struggled with "right." He said:

*For the good that I will to do, I do not do; but the evil I will not to do, that I practice.*

Romans 7:19

Paul had one thing in his spirit and another thing in his mind. Most of us have experienced this, and it's very frustrating. When you know God and love Him and want to do what is pleasing and "right" in His sight, you sometimes find yourself at the end of the day wondering how to get the things you know in your heart are "right" to take hold in your mind and your body, so that you can do them. This gives place to a constant spiritual struggle.

Your spirit connects with God and you see where He is trying to take you, but something seems to hold you back. Something within you refuses to release you to follow Him fully.

This may well be the reason we have been in an unfamiliar season and have had to endure some "crazy" things. We're having to pass through trials, temptations, and situations we didn't see coming. "Why would God allow this in my life?" we ask ourselves. It is because God is trying to move us into a higher place, and the enemy is determined that it wouldn't happen.

Another reason is that our perspective has been wrong. We thought we would just get more and more of this world's goods, but God is intent on getting more of us. When you give God more of you, then more of what He has will automatically come to you. Just as Jesus said:

*But seek first the kingdom of God and His righteousness, and all these things shall be added to you.*

Matthew 6:33

We want the "things," but we don't want the spiritual quest that comes with getting them. God said that if we would seek Him, He would give us the "things" we need.

When you make a decision to start doing the "right" thing, to start living a righteous life, the enemy will fight you as never before. He knows that God does certain things for the righteous that He doesn't do for anyone else. Satan loves it when you experience lack in your life, and he doesn't want to see you move into a place of divine supply.

## GOD'S DEMAND FOR RIGHTEOUSNESS

But, struggle or not, God is demanding righteousness of us. This being true, why is it that so few are preaching about righteousness and holiness these days. Quoting Isaiah 52:11 and Ezekiel 20:34 and 41, Paul wrote:

*We want the "things," but we don't want the spiritual quest that comes with getting them.*

> *Therefore "Come out from among them and be separate, says the Lord. Do not touch what is unclean, and I will receive you." "I will be a Father to you, and you shall be My sons and daughters, says the Lord Almighty."*
>
> 2 Corinthians 6:17-18

Peter wrote:

*But you are a chosen generation, a royal priesthood, a holy nation, His own special people, that you may proclaim the praises of Him who called you out of darkness into His marvelous light.*

1 Peter 2:9

If you're popular, it may mean that you are just like everyone else, and that's not pleasing to God. He made you to be "peculiar." Peculiar people stand alone. They could compromise, but they refuse to do it. They could lower themselves to the level of others, but they refuse to do it. Doing what is "right" may not be natural or normal, but it is necessary, and the time is now.

God didn't call us to be like everyone else. He has called us to be His servants, and any servant is dedicated to the instructions of his master, not to his own wishes.

Man lost his original "rightness" through sin, but it can be restored to each of us through salvation in Christ. Then, with Him as our Savior, it's time to start *Doing "Right" in a Wrong World.*

# CHAPTER 4

# Respected Men and Women of the Bible Who Did "Good" but Not "Right"

*So Abram departed as the Lord had spoken to him, and Lot went with him.*

Genesis 12:4

If you've been struggling with the need to do "right" and not just "good," you're not alone. The Bible records the stories of a number of men and women we have admired, but who experienced this very same struggle. Prominent among them was Abraham, the very father of our faith.

## ABRAHAM'S STRUGGLE WITH "RIGHT"

One example of Abraham's struggle to do "right" is found in the story of his call by God to leave his land and his people and embark on an exciting journey that would lead to the formation of a holy nation with an eternal destiny:

*Now the Lord had said to Abram: "Get out of your country, from your family and from your father's house, to a land that I will show you. I will make you a great nation; I will bless you and make your name great; and you shall be a blessing. I will bless those who bless you, and I will curse him who curses you; and in you all the families of the earth shall be blessed."*

Genesis 12:1-4

Abraham obeyed God—in a measure: *"So Abram departed as the LORD had spoken to him."* So far, so good. But then the last four words of verse four indicate a problem: *"Lot went with him."* These are not good words, because that's not what God told Abraham to do.

There was much good in Abraham's actions. It was a "good" thing, for instance, that he packed up his belongings and started making a move toward the Promised Land. Leaving his country was one of the demands God had made on him.

And, yet, as much "good" as he did, Abraham did not fully do the "right" thing. The Lord had told him to leave his country *and* his family. Instead of fully obeying the Lord, he took with him his nephew Lot.

Abraham was guilty of doing what many of us have done from time to time. We hear from God, but then we take it upon ourselves to modify His instructions to suit our own purposes and concepts, and that is always a dangerous thing to do. Anytime you modify the instruction given to you by God (even if what you're doing seems to be a "good" thing), you cannot hope for a proper result. You cannot do a "good" thing and expect to get a "right" result.

If you're doing a "good" thing, you may indeed get "good" results, but the only way you can get a "right" result is by doing the "right" thing. You must not only do the "right" thing, but you must do it at the "right" time and with the "right" spirit.

That area of "rightness" is where God is trying to bring us today. He's trying to move us this very moment from goodness to righteousness. Please cooperate with Him, and you'll be so glad you did.

If Abraham had done what was "right," meaning what God told him to do, what was pleasing to God, wonderful things would have happened. This was the promise of verses two and three. But these wonderful things were contingent upon the requirements of verse one. If Abram had done "right," he could have claimed every one of the promises. If not, all bets were off, as we say.

As it turned out, taking Lot along caused Abraham and Sarah many problems. If Lot had not gone along, they might have avoided the evils that befell them at Sodom and Gomorra, where Abraham was forced to intercede before God for his nephew. They might have avoided the curse that came upon Lot's wife. When will we learn the importance of doing "right"? Your life could be so much better if you would obey God fully.

## JONAH'S STRUGGLE WITH "RIGHT"

The story of the prophet Jonah has been familiar to most of us since childhood. God called him to go preach in Nineveh, but because he didn't like the people of Nineveh and didn't think them worthy of God's blessing, rather than go there and preach to them, he boarded a ship going in the opposite direction. Of course, the rest (as they say) is history.

A terrible storm arose at sea, and to save the ship Jonah was traveling on and its other occupants, he had to be cast overboard. He was then swallowed by a great fish and had to spend three days of torment in the fish's stomach.

To Jonah, being in the belly of the great fish was a lot like actually being in hell. Seaweed wrapped itself around his neck, gastric juices burned his flesh, and he wondered if there was any hope at all for him. In that terrible situation, he repented for not having obeyed God. God heard Jonah, and eventually the fish vomited him out on the land.

This was a great miracle, one that has inspired generation after generation. Having received this wonderful deliverance, Jonah relented and went to Nineveh, preaching to the people there, and bringing blessing to them and their city. The entire story is recorded in the four chapters of the book of Jonah, and the message of that little Old Testament book has impacted people the world over for centuries now.

What can we learn from all of this? It was a "good" thing that Jonah eventually did repent and go to Nineveh as God had told him to do in the beginning, but the "right" thing to do would have been to go when God told him to go. If he had done that, he would not have placed in jeopardy the lives of so many people aboard the ship he had to be thrown out of, he would have avoided much personal suffering, he would have avoided the tragic loss of time, and he would have brought blessing to Nineveh and her people much sooner.

This is a lesson we cannot afford to miss. Anytime you or I insist on doing our own thing (however "good" it may seem to us at the time) rather than the "right" thing (whatever it is that God has required of us), it will not only negatively impact us; it will also negatively impact many others around us.

*Obedience to God brings blessing, delayed obedience brings delayed blessing, and disobedience brings disaster.*

The unusual circumstances of Jonah's ordeal must not be allowed to override the important message of his story. Obedience to God brings blessing, delayed obedience brings delayed blessing, and disobedience brings disaster. "Good" is never a substitute for "right."

When you refuse to do what is "right," you become a magnet for tragedy. Some of the things you have suffered in recent years were unnecessary. If you had done what was "right," you might have been able to avoid them entirely.

## KING SAUL'S STRUGGLE WITH "RIGHT"

One day God gave Saul, the man He had chosen and anointed as the first king over Israel, very specific instructions about dealing with certain of his enemies. Saul knew God's voice, and the words God spoke to him were clear and precise. Nevertheless Saul chose to disobey.

The command from God had been this:

*Now go and attack Amalek, and utterly destroy all that they have, and do not spare them. But kill both man and woman, infant and nursing child, ox and sheep, camel and donkey.*

1 Samuel 15:3

Somehow these instructions didn't seem to make sense to Saul, so he decided to modify them. What he did—saving certain animals to be used in sacrifice to God (or so he said) and sparing certain pagan kings—seemed "good." But Saul did not do the "right" thing, and God was angry with him.

It seems rather apparent that Saul spared the hated King Agag so that he could use him in a public relations campaign. In those days, when one king overthrew another, it added to his kingship, to his prestige, and to his wealth.

And, of course, it made him look good. What Saul was really doing was taking the spotlight off of God and putting it on himself, and that is self-righteousness.

What Saul did may have seemed "good" to the men and women around him, but God considered his actions to be wicked, rebellious, and hateful. What the king had done did not conform to God's sense of justice, and God is God. He knows what He wants, and He knows why He wants it, so who are we to challenge His wisdom? When we question or challenge God's wisdom, it is a very serious offense to the Creator of the universe.

In the case of King Saul, God fired him that very day. Saul would remain at his post for a short while, but his power was stripped from him, and he was no longer the great king he had been.

This whole scene created a lot of inner turmoil for Saul, and an evil spirit began to torment him. When this happened, he called for someone who might be able to help him find relief from the torment of the evil spirit, and the man God sent to help him was none other than his replacement—the young David.

David was called upon to come to Saul's aid because it was widely known that when he played his harp, an anointing came that destroyed yokes and drove away evil spirits. In Saul's case, it worked. When David played, Saul found relief. David was in the "right" place at the "right" time, with the "right" spirit, and things began to happen for him. Eventually he became king in Saul's stead.

Don't ever be guilty of doing what Saul did. Whatever you do, don't risk losing the anointing on your life and being turned over to evil spirits. If you do "good" things, you can get "good" results. But if you do the "right" thing, you will get the "right" result, the one God desires.

When Saul disobeyed God in this seemingly "good" way, God spoke to Samuel:

*I greatly regret that I have set up Saul as king, for he has turned back from following Me, and has not performed My commandments.*

1 Samuel 15:11

Then God sent Samuel to reprove Saul and to begin the search for his replacement.

And what good was Saul's position after it became empty? A position without the power to back up that position is meaningless. You can have the position; give me the power every time.

God demands to have the "right" people in the "right" place at the "right" time, and if you contend for righteousness, He may prepare you to replace someone who is about to come down because of arrogance against God. Jesus said:

*But many who are first will be last, and the last first.*

Matthew 19:30

You don't have to "kiss up" to anyone, you don't have to sleep your way to the top, and you don't have to lower your standards in any way to gain advantage. Do what's "right," and God will open doors for you.

It's time to be "right." It doesn't matter how long you've been in God, how much faith you've demonstrated, or how many wonderful things you've seen. God demands righteousness of great and small alike.

Stop worrying about what everyone else is doing. You be where you're supposed to be and do what you're supposed to be doing, and let others take care of themselves. You can't answer for them, and they can't answer for you. And you must not use the excuse of others not living up to the right standards to lower your own standards.

Some of you have been praying and asking the Lord why it is that you seem to take one step forward and two steps backward. He wants you to know that it's because the devil hates you so much. You're destined for greatness. Do the "right" thing, and God will bring your destiny to pass.

You don't have to make it happen; God will make it happen for you. You don't have to worry about what people think and say; God will move them out of the way.

The Lord will give you the right contacts, the right clientele, and the right employees, and you will begin to live your dream. Get out of the boat and start taking some steps, and you'll quickly realize that you can walk on water.

But as you do, don't compromise. Give the Lord full obedience, and you will be amazed at what He does in and through you.

## MOSES' STRUGGLE WITH "RIGHT"

Few people in history experienced as many miracles as Moses did. But on at least one occasion, he settled for second best, and it cost him dearly.

If was good that Moses believed God could send water from a rock, but it was not good that he didn't do exactly what God told him to do to get it. His mistake was to allow the complaining people to get on his nerves and cause him to act precipitously. That's always a mistake.

God told Moses to speak to the rock, but Moses chose to strike it. He got the water they all needed, but God wasn't pleased with his method.

That one act caused Moses to miss the Promised Land. He could see it, but he couldn't go in. The children of Israel would still go into it and possess it, but someone else would have to lead them. When you settle for what is "good" instead of contending for what is "right," you just might miss your Promised Land too.

And you can't afford to miss it. You've come too far to turn back now. You've been through too much to miss the blessing intended for you. You are so close to your promise now that you could reach out and touch it, but the devil knows that too. So he's doing everything he can to keep you from it. If God could just get you in a season of doing what's "right," He could quickly take you to the other side. When you take that final step, from here into there, blessings will come to you from every quarter, but your challenge is to do the "right" thing at the moment.

Living "right" puts you into a category all your own, and you suddenly don't have nearly as many friends. This troubles some of us. We have people upon whom we like to lean, but are the people we lean on worth our missing out on God's very best for our lives? It's time for obedience to God—whatever the cost.

## CAIN'S STRUGGLE WITH "RIGHT"

As we saw in a previous chapter, the brothers Cain and Abel both brought offerings to God. Cain brought a "good" offering, something that most of us would have considered perfectly acceptable, and yet God rejected his offering. Because Abel's offering had been received and his had not, Cain was enraged and rose up and killed his brother. This was the first murder recorded in the Bible, and it happened because of a flawed offering.

Many people have learned to be blessed through giving, but a "good" offering can only produce a "good" result, not a "right" one. God has promised to open the windows of heaven over those who obey Him in this regard:

*"Bring all the tithes into the storehouse, that there may be food in My house, and try Me now in this," Says the Lord of hosts, "If I will not open for you the windows of heaven and pour out for you such blessing that there will not be room enough to receive it."*

Malachi 3:10

But the windows of heaven will not open over those who choose to do what is "good" rather than what is "right." God is bound by His Word, and it is only when you fully obey His Word, doing what is "right," that He can bless you as He desires.

When some people give to God, they measure their gift against the average given by others, and they think they have done well. What they gave may well be a "good" offering. But, when you give, it must never be based on what others give, but on the measure in which God has blessed you and on what God has specifically spoken to you to give.

Many people give "good" offerings, and yet those offerings do not add up to a tithe on their income. The Bible calls that robbing God. It may be "good" in man's sight, but it's certainly not right.

A lot of people look good while they're giving their offering to God, but that doesn't make the offering itself "right." This is sad because it causes men and women to miss what God has promised.

When you dedicate yourself to righteous living, God will cause your enemies to fall at your feet, and you will use them as a footstool or a stepping stone. God will open doors for you and make ways for you—just because you have done the "right" thing. This is just as true about our giving as it is about any other aspect of our lives. When God speaks to you to give a special offering, and He tells you exactly how much to give, how can you do any less?

## THE DISCIPLES' STRUGGLE WITH "RIGHT"

Abraham, Jonah, Saul, Moses, and Cain and Abel were all men of the Old Testament, but what about the believers of the New Testament? Did they always do what was "right"? Unfortunately, they didn't.

Even the disciples of Jesus erred in this regard. They thought they knew so much, but they had a lot to learn.

Once, as the Lord was in the process of calling them to greatness, He told them to launch out into the deep and let down their nets (see Luke 5:4). "We have fished all night long and caught nothing," they said to Him with an air of authority based on long experience. But did they know more than Jesus, who had been with the Father the day the worlds were formed.

"Launch out into the deep," Jesus commanded.

They did this, but they seemed to do it more out of respect for Him as a great teacher than for any other reason. They thought they knew what the result would be.

*How many blessings have slipped through your fingertips?*

"Now let down your nets," Jesus said to them.

Their response was tempered. They let down one net, but then they stopped. They were sure that this one net would prove their point. The fish were not running that day.

Letting that net down was a "good" thing to do, but it certainly wasn't the "right" thing to do. It was obedience to a point, but it was not complete obedience.

But Jesus had something He wanted to show them. He was God, and if they chose to follow Him, trusting Him for everything and obeying His every command, they would change the world and affect the lives of untold millions of people. It was these humble fishermen who would write much of the New Testament. They would become the apostles of the first century and be respected and admired throughout all ages to come.

They must learn what full obedience to God could bring. So suddenly the one net they had let down was so full that they could not draw it in. It was a strong net, but it couldn't contain the catch that came to it now. The net broke, and fish began spilling back into the sea.

And that wasn't the half of it. There were many more fish that should have been caught that day, but because the disciples had offered only partial obedience, they could receive only a partial blessing.

How many fish have you been losing? How many blessings have slipped through your fingertips? It's time for complete obedience to God, and when you give it, you will learn, perhaps for the very first time, what complete blessing looks like.

Large numbers of fish have been in the vicinity of your boat, and you didn't even know it. God knew it, but He couldn't command them to come to you because you hadn't placed yourself in the position to receive them.

When we think of this story of the disciples and their miraculous drought of fishes, we think of it in a very positive way. They received a miracle that day. Yes, that's true. But they could have had a much larger miracle. They could have had many more fish to show for their efforts. God is waiting for your complete obedience. He's waiting to see you *Doing "Right" in a Wrong World.*

# CHAPTER 5

# Developing "Right" Thinking

*But even if our gospel is veiled [hidden], it is veiled to those who are per-*
*ishing [dying], whose minds the god of this age has blinded, who do not*
*believe, lest the light of the gospel of the glory of Christ, who is the image*
*of God, should shine on them. For we do not preach ourselves, but we*
*preach Christ Jesus the Lord, and ourselves, your servants for Jesus' sake.*
*For it is the God who commanded light to shine out of darkness who has*
*shown in our hearts to give the light of the knowledge of the glory of God*
*in the face of Jesus Christ.*

2 Corinthians 4:3-6

"**W**hose minds *the god of this world has blinded.*" Satan, the god of this world and god of this world's systems, has the ability to blind men's minds. As a result, many are perishing around us today. It is because this mind blinder, Satan, the devil, has corrupted their minds and caused them not to be able to see the truth. They, therefore, cannot receive the light of the glorious Gospel of Jesus Christ, and instead, they embrace lies that lead them astray, away from God's blessings.

It should be obvious to any enlightened observer that we're living in a world gone wild. It is shocking, for instance, that here in America we are now voting on whether or not to legalize same-sex marriages. This is madness, but it is the type of madness that is prevalent in our modern world.

The corrupted systems of this world have brought us to this place, and it has happened because the minds of many people are blinded. They cannot see the difference between right and wrong. Their thought life is dominated by evil, hate, and greed.

When God sent the flood to destroy the ancient world, it was because He "*saw*" the wickedness of man:

*Then the Lord saw that the wickedness of man was great in the earth, and that every intent of the thoughts of his heart was only evil continually.*

Genesis 6:5

That sounds to me very much like what we're experiencing in our modern world, and the most alarming part of it is that in Noah's time, God's response was to literally wipe the people off of the face of the earth. They were swept away in the flood.

So this is a serious issue, and that is the reason Satan constantly attacks the minds of righteous people. He doesn't let us rest when we go to church. He doesn't let us alone so that we can sleep in peace at night. He doesn't stop tormenting us when we're at work. He is relentless in his attack on our minds. If he can distort our thinking, he can win the battle. So we need to develop "right" thinking.

## THE HUMAN MIND IS THE BATTLEFIELD OF LIFE

What was behind the madness of Genesis 6? The Scriptures show us:

*There were giants on the earth in those days, and also afterward, when the sons of God came in to the daughters of men and they bore children to them. Those were the mighty men who were of old, men of renown. Then the Lord saw that the wickedness of man was great in the earth, and that every intent of the thoughts of his heart was only evil continually. And the Lord was sorry that He had made man on the earth, and He was grieved in His heart. So the Lord said, "I will destroy man whom I have created from the face of the earth, both man and beast, creeping thing and birds of the air, for I am sorry that I have made them."*

Genesis 6:4-7

Why was God so grieved? Because the actions of men in that day were consistently selfish and evil because their minds were corrupted. Man's thought life was mixed up, "messed up," perverted. Man was doing whatever he wanted to do, whatever seemed right in his own eyes, without regard for consequences. And God could not permit that.

The human mind is a battlefield on which good meets evil, God meets the devil. Both want control of your mind because the Scriptures declare:

*For as he [man] thinks in his heart, so is he.*

Proverbs 23:7

So the god of this world, the enemy of our souls, the blinder of men's minds, works very hard to deceive, divert, and darken the thoughts of man's mind. Most of all, he is intent upon preventing them from believing the Gospel and being saved. To achieve that end, he twists and distorts their thoughts until black seems to them to be white, and white seems to be black. Right seems to be wrong, and wrong seems to be right. Consequently, they do not believe God's Word, and the light of the Gospel of the glory of Christ, who is the image of God, cannot shine on them. The problem is not a lack of intelligence; it is a blinded mind.

This is a struggle that even professing Christians face, but all is not lost. There is a way to get control of your thought life. The first step in doing so is to gain an understanding of what I have come to call the Salvation Factor.

## THE SALVATION FACTOR

This truth is based on 2 Corinthians 4:4: *"Whose minds the god of this age has blinded, who do not believe, lest the light of the gospel of the glory of Christ, who is the image of God, should shine on them."* The devil works hard to pull a veil of darkness over our minds, and, as a result, many of us live beneath our God-given potentials and abilities. If we can gain control over our minds, his attempts will fail.

There's a difference between your mind and your brain. Psychologists may debate this point, but the Scriptures clearly define it. The brain is the organ with which your mind thinks.

It's a lot like an organist, a musician, or pianist, and their relationship to the instrument they play. They use a keyboard, a piano, an organ, or some other musical instrument, and the instrument is like their brain. The mind that uses it is equivalent to the musician, and it is the musician who determines what comes out of the instrument.

For instance, if I were to attempt to play the same instrument played by a skilled maestro, the sounds I made would not be nearly as pleasant to listen to. Who is playing a given instrument makes all the difference in the world.

The most dangerous person in the world, therefore, is the person who has a bad mind, but a good brain. And there are people exactly like that. Their bad mind uses their good brain to do all sorts of mischief.

Christians should understand this point. When you were saved, you didn't get a new brain. You got a renewed mind. It is that mind that controls everything about you.

The story is told of Bear Bryant, the former coach of the Alabama football team, the Crimson Tide. During the final two minutes of a key game, Coach Bryant's team was up a few points, and they had the ball and a first down on their opponent's twenty-yard line. Then, suddenly, their starting quarterback was injured.

Coach Bryant called on the second-string quarterback to take over the offense, but he warned him before he sent him into the game, "Whatever you do, don't put the ball in the air. Do you understand me, son?

"Don't throw the ball. Run the ball, and try to run out the clock. If you score, or the ball is turned over to them on downs, then we'll depend on our defense to keep us in the game."

The young quarterback said he understood. With the first snap of the ball, he tried a running play, but it was stopped at the line of scrimmage. Then, on the second play of the series, he was not only stopped; he suddenly found himself in trouble. His defense collapsed around him while he was still in the pocket, and he was in danger of being sacked. What should he do?

Spotting a wide receiver standing in the end zone, he reasoned with himself, "I know that Coach said not to throw the ball, but the man is wide open. This is so easy that I've got to do it. I can put the ball right into his hands." And so, against his coach's advice, the young quarterback drew back his arm and fired the ball into the end zone.

He was about ready to begin rejoicing when an all-pro safety on the other team came out of nowhere, snatched the ball out of the air, and ran down the field for what looked like an easy touchdown. This young quarterback was about to lose the game for his team and his coach, and he knew how serious that was. His world was about to fall apart.

*In this all-important season of your life, it's not about doing; it's about being, about becoming.*

He suddenly realized that he was the only player with any hope of catching the opposing safety and preventing the score. Although he was not known as a good runner, he now ran for all he was worth. With superhuman effort, he caught the sprinting safety at the two-yard line and brought him down, barely preventing the score. Before another play could be organized, the buzzer sounded, and the game was saved for Alabama. Whew! That had been a close one!

Later that day, the two coaches were discussing the game. The coach from the opposing team said to Coach Bryant, "It doesn't make sense that your second-string quarterback caught my all-pro safety. According to his stats, he's slow. How is it that he caught the fastest man on our team?"

Coach Bear Bryant's answer showed his wisdom. "What you don't understand," he responded, "is that your guy was running for six points, but our guy was running for his life. That made all the difference." Something had taken over in the mind of that young quarterback and changed him into the runner he had never been.

Your mind is powerful, and it can take you where you need to go—if you can get control of it. The devil knows this too, and that's why he fights all the more furiously to take you down.

In this all-important season of your life, it's not about doing; it's about being, about becoming. The enemy is not fighting you because of who you are; he's fighting you because of who you have the potential to become through Christ. This is what I mean by the Salvation Factor.

## THE SINCERITY FACTOR

Next, you must understand the Sincerity Factor. This truth is based on 2 Corinthians 11:2. Here, Paul, speaking as a spiritual father, began by writing:

*For I am jealous for you with godly jealousy.*

2 Corinthians 11:2

This kind of jealousy, godly jealousy, is appropriate for the believer. It's okay for a husband to have godly jealousy for his wife. He should have it. And she should have godly jealousy for him. We should all have this godly jealousy in regard to the church and spiritual matters.

What more did Paul say?

*For I have betrothed you to one husband, that I may present you as a chaste [pure] virgin to Christ. But I fear, lest somehow, as the serpent deceived Eve by his craftiness, so your minds may be corrupted from the simplicity that is in Christ.*

2 Corinthians 11:2-3

This word *simplicity* is the key to understanding this passage. Here, *simplicity* means "a single-minded devotion." It means to be sold out to God. The reason so many of us are experiencing mental torment is that we have not yet embraced the simplicity of the Gospel. Jesus has not yet become our single-minded devotion.

The fact that you're saved doesn't mean that you'll no longer have spiritual battles. Just because you're now on the Lord's side doesn't mean that you will never again have to fight off thoughts that the enemy brings against you. If anything, his attacks will become even more intensive. He's intent on taking control of your mind.

Both God and Satan are looking for yielded vessels. Every time someone new comes into your life, you should stop and ask the question, "Who sent this person?" If God didn't send them, then you know who did.

Not everyone who smiles at you is your friend. Not everyone who pats you on the back genuinely wants to see you go forward. If you will be single-minded for the Lord and spend more time with Him, He will give you a keen sense of discernment about people's true intentions. Some people want to get close to you just so that they can misuse and abuse you.

Most people will stick with you just as long as they're getting something from you. The moment they feel that they can no longer take advantage of

your goodness, they'll turn on you. You were there for them when they needed you, but when you suddenly need them, they're nowhere to be found.

It's important for you to become totally dependent upon God, and trust
Him to send people to you if and when you need them. If you become dependant upon people, they will fail you every time. Let God show you who's who
and what's what. The Holy Spirit has a way of alerting us to this type of danger.

On a recent trip home from Panama, I had to go through a metal detector in the Miami Airport. I thought I had removed everything that might set
it off, but when I passed through the machine, it beeped anyway. "I'm sorry,
sir," the attendant said, "You'll have to go back through again."

"I don't think I have anything else to take off," I said.

"There has to be some metal somewhere," he insisted. "Try it again."

I tried it again, and it did the same thing. He motioned me back through
again.

"I'm glad I'm on time for this flight," I said, "but I still don't think I have
anything that would be setting this machine off."

"Check all your pockets again," he suggested. I did, and in my back pocket, I found a key.

"Uh-huh!" he said, reaching for it. "Now walk through." This time I was
clean, and the machine was silent.

As I made my way to my gate that day, the Spirit spoke to me. "There was
something on you, something that could not be detected with the naked eye,
something unknown to you, but the metal detector was able to pick up on it.
This is the same work I'm doing in your life. When you stand before those who
mean you harm, I will always warn you."

Sometimes we might feel cautious around people we've grown up with. It
doesn't make sense in the natural, but the Spirit is warning us about something, and we should heed His warning. At some point, down the road, we will
learn of their treachery. The Holy Spirit knew it all along.

A friend is someone who can rejoice when God is blessing you. If a person
you thought was a friend suddenly becomes jealous, then they were never your
friend in the first place. When you hear the Holy Spirit's beeps, you had better heed them.

You might be sitting next to someone in church, and they have their hands raised as if in praise to God, and suddenly you hear the subtle beeping in your spirit. Don't reject it.

All that glitters is not gold, and this is all the more reason you must have a single-minded devotion to God. In this way, you'll be able to go through whatever life throws your way—whether others are there to encourage you or not. When David could find no one to encourage him, he encouraged himself in the Lord (see 1 Samuel 30:6).

Stop trying to live to please other people. We have far too many Christians who prefer to be popular than to be peculiar, as God has called us to be. If you are single-minded for God, your coworkers will be able to say of you, "I can't figure her out. Despite all that she has to go through, she always maintains a good attitude. I've never seen her when she didn't have a smile on her face." That's a real testimony.

Then, when you go to church, you can get back at the devil. Let him know, "All week long you've been 'messing with' me, but now I'm going to 'mess with' you." And as you begin to praise God, you not only please the Lord; you send the enemy fleeing in terror. God loves your praise, but Satan hates it with a passion.

When you have your mind "right," meaning when it's single toward God, when you are understanding the simplicity of God, you will say to Him, "God, I don't know why I'm going through this particular trial, but I'm going to trust You anyway. And I'm going to stand firm." When you do that, God blesses you every time.

He often blesses you in front of those who don't like you. In fact, sometimes He uses people who don't like you to do the blessing. And they can't understand why they're even blessing you. It's okay. Just let them do it.

It's time to get your mind "right" because this is no time for games. God is about to take you where you've never been before, and you need to get ready for it. This is your season. Get your thought life under control so that you'll be ready to move with God.

Say to God, "I don't know why I'm going through this period of trial, but the one thing I do know is that You're faithful. You have never let me down, You've always made a way for me, and You've always opened the doors I need-ed. I don't know how You will bless me this time, and I don't know when, but

I'm determined to be ready when that time comes." Your blessing will come because you have a strong mind, one set on "right" thinking.

Your destiny is too high for you to be living so low. There's so much more that God has in store for you. He's saying to you today, "Who will trust me? Who will take Me at My Word?"

We often become so frustrated and confused in our minds that we start walking through man-made doors instead of waiting for God to open the doors He wants for us. This is bad for several reasons: (1) If a man opens a door for you, he will never let you forget it. (2) When a door is opened by man, it may not lead to your real destiny in life. (3) Man-made doors often lead us away from God's will, not toward it. And, (4) If a man

*Your destiny is too high for you to be living so low.*

opens a door for you, he can later change his mind and shut it in your face. When God opens a door, it stays open—whether others like it or not.

The enemy will do anything to prevent you from having an understanding of salvation. He will do anything to prevent you from having an understanding of sincerity. If you don't know who you are, he'll try to define you.

Often, he'll do this through people. So stop living for people, and start living for God. If someone doesn't like you the way you are, that's not your problem; it's their problem. And you need to make up your mind not to change for anybody.

When you worship God, don't worry about what anyone else thinks about it. You're not trying to get their attention. It's God's attention you want. Praise Him wherever you happen to be at the moment and think on His goodness.

If there is any one thing the devil doesn't want you to have, it's a strong mind. He fears what you can become when you know who you are in God.

Isaiah knew this secret. He said:

*You will keep him in perfect peace, whose mind is stayed on You, because he trusts in You.*

Isaiah 26:3

If you've ever been to a circus, you may have seen an elephant restrained by a small chain about its leg. Ironically, this chain is fastened to a small peg in the ground. As the elephant goes about eating its meal, it moves only as far as the chain allows. When I first saw that, I thought, "Wait a minute! That elephant can move a house. How could that little chain and stake hold it?"

The secret is that when the elephant was smaller, it was chained to something much more substantial that it really could not move. Now that he's older, he's a lot stronger, but although there's no lock on that chain and nothing substantial is holding it, there's a lock on his mind. He's convinced that he cannot move further, so he can't.

Some of you are chained to situations you could have broken free from long ago. The Bible declares:

*And you shall know the truth, and the truth shall make you free.*

John 8:32

So what are you waiting for? You have the power to snatch that stake out of the ground. Do it. Get free of every chain that has held you back. You've been restricted far too long.

You deserve the very best, and you were destined to be on top. God wants you to be the lender, not the borrower. It's time for you to get ready for His blessings by freeing your mind. You're coming out with victory because of the promise of God's Word:

*You are of God, little children, and have overcome them, because He who is in you is greater than he who is in the world.*

1 John 4:4

It's time to beak any chain and to pull out any stake that's been holding you back. Get control of your thought life.

## THE STRONGHOLD FACTOR

Understand the Salvation Factor, understand the Sincerity Factor, and then understand the Stronghold Factor. What do I mean by "the Stronghold Factor"? The Scriptures declare:

*For though we walk in the flesh, we do not war according to the flesh. For the weapons of our warfare are not carnal but mighty in God for pulling down strongholds.*

2 Corinthians 10:3-4

A stronghold is a mindset, a strongly established pattern of thinking. When you have a stronghold in your mind, you accept a situation as being unchangeable even though you know God and His power to change things.

All of us need the mental ability to persevere against the odds. It doesn't matter what side of the tracks you were born on. The secret of success, the spirit of creativity, is in you. It just needs to be released through "right" thinking.

As strongholds develop in our thought systems, they become a fortress warring against God and His truth. This is all the result of the devil using your mind as his battlefield.

Some of you who are reading this book may be bound by strongholds such as compulsiveness. You may do something crazy, without any thought as to why you're doing it. You just do it without bothering to weigh the pros and cons of a situation. You just act compulsively, and in the process you sometimes lose in a minute what it has taken you years to build up.

Your obsession may be something else. What is it that's always on your mind? What is it that could be described as "all you can think about"? Is there fear in your spirit? Or bitterness or resentment? Are you bound by uncontrollable lusts? Do you have actual phobias? Are you filled with distrust? It's time to get your mind in shape, to bring it into conformity with the Word of God. It's time to think "right" thoughts.

Carnal minds must be converted, and even converted minds can become corrupted. Any mind that has been corrupted must be conquered.

In setting about to accomplish this, the weapons we use must not be carnal, physical, or fleshly. You can't fight this war, for example, with education.

I'm not against education. Education is good, but gaining book knowledge will not set you free from Satan's strongholds. Only Holy Spirit knowledge can do that.

Paul insisted, *"For the weapons of our warfare are not carnal."* Our weapons are not physical. They're not fleshly. They're not man-made. Psychology will not free you from Satan's strongholds. Studying Darwin, Pavlov, and Freud will not do it. What you need is not merely the power of positive thinking or what is being called transitory meditation.

Be careful of the many trends that purport to give you mind power. You may be connecting with something, but what you're connecting with may be dangerous. The world is full of evil spirits.

This is another reason we must govern well our children and what influences their lives. This is not an old-fashioned and out-of-date idea. We're responsible for what they watch and listen to. Don't ever believe that listening to lewd and degrading lyrics will have no detrimental effect on your children. What they hear will take root in their subconscious minds, and they will have difficulty ridding themselves of it at some later time.

When women dance to music that has morally degrading and abusive lyrics, they come to believe that what is being expressed in the songs is normal behavior on the part of men. Later, when they meet someone they like and they're treated badly, they won't know that it's unacceptable behavior.

No wonder our young people are being destroyed! Look what they're listening to on a regular basis. And parents are saying that they just don't have time to spend with their children, so those children do what they like when they like and with whom they like. This is a travesty, and each of us will answer to God for our part in it.

Many parents don't know where their children are, who they're with, or what they're having to deal with at the moment. Their minds are somewhere else entirely. If God has given us children, then it's time for us to wake up and decide to raise those children properly. No one else will do it for us.

Understand well this Stronghold Factor.

## THE SURRENDER FACTOR

In the Surrender Factor, we begin to choose our thoughts in the same way we choose our friends. With friends, you usually know who you want to be bothered with and who you don't want to be bothered with. If someone calls you, and you don't want to be bothered with them, you know what to do. You look at the caller ID, and when you know that it's this person calling, you ignore the call.

That's exactly the way we must be with our thoughts. When the devil sends you a thought, tell him, "Look, I don't feel like being bothered with this. I'm not about to entertain your negativity."

The devil tells you, for instance, that things will never get better, but you should know that everything he says is a lie. There's no truth in him. So if he says that you're going under, you should be able to shout praises to God because that's a sure sign that you're going over.

If the devil says that your situation will not change, it's time to rejoice because change is just around the corner. Your miracle is just down the street. Your breakthrough is just next door.

If you've been wondering why it seems that everyone else has been getting their breakthrough and God has forgotten about you, let me give you some good news. God always saves the best until last. That must mean that you're going to get the best. Start rejoicing for what is coming your way.

> *If the devil says that your situation will not change, it's time to rejoice because change is just around the corner.*

Get your thinking under control, and everything else in your life will fall into place. When your church is open for a Bible study, you need to be there. Get God's thoughts in your mind, and they will begin to come out of your mouth. You've had some wrong thinking, and that has resulted in some bad things coming to your life.

If you want to know what's in a person's heart, just listen to what comes out of their mouth. Whatever is inside will eventually come out. If their heart is filled with negativity, that's what will come out of their mouth. You hate to see some people coming because you already know what to expect from them.

Some people only speak gossip, and so you already know what's coming out of their mouth before they speak. Why is it that some people feel they can dump just about anything on you? Don't they know where trash belongs?

You have to make a decision not to be part of their treachery. This is not the season to be popular; it's the season to be peculiar. This is not the season to fit in; it's the season to stand out, to stand by yourself—if necessary.

God is at work in your life right now as you read these words, and your thinking is being changed. What used to excite you will no longer excite you. You're growing up, and in the process of growing up, you're changing.

Count the cost. Jesus said:

> *For which of you, intending to build a tower, does not sit down first and count the cost, whether he has enough to finish it—lest, after he has laid*

*the foundation, and is not able to finish, all who see it begin to mock him, saying, "This man began to build and was not able to finish."*

Luke 14:28-30

I have made a determination in my own life not to be part of anything that is not attached to eternity, and I urge you to make the same determination. Don't waste your time with things you know will not last. Don't stay in a relationship when you know the other person is not right for you. You're not only wasting your time; you're also blocking your intended blessing. God wants to send you Mr. Right (or Miss Right), so stop settling for Mr. Right-Now (or Miss Right-Now). You're hindering the person who is anointed to join themselves to you eventually.

Above all, get control of your thought life and begin to develop "right" thinking, righteous thinking. This, more than anything else, will enable you to move beyond mere goodness and to begin *Doing "Right" in a Wrong World.*

# CHAPTER 6

# Developing "Right" Attitudes

*Rejoice in the Lord always. Again I will say, rejoice! Let your gentleness be known to all men. The Lord is at hand. Be anxious for nothing, but in everything by prayer and supplication, with thanksgiving, let your requests be made known to God; and the peace of God, which surpasses all understanding will guard your hearts and your minds through Christ Jesus.*

*Finally, brethren, whatever things are true, whatever things are noble, whatever things are just, whatever things are pure, whatever things are lovely, whatever things are of good report, if there is any virtue and if there is anything praiseworthy—meditate [think or ponder] on these things. The things which you learned and received and heard and saw in me, those do, and the God of peace will be with you.*

Philippians 4:4-9

In order to return to a state of rightness with God, you must develop "right" attitudes. You will never be able to live "right" as long as you have wrong attitudes. This is true for every circumstance and situation you may experience in life. It's time for a checkup from the neck up because what goes on in your head affects your whole body and everything that is associated with it.

Knowing what the Word of God says about "right" attitudes can enable you to deal with depression, anger, resentment, worry, and fear. These are enemies that many of us battle on a daily basis. This fact alone should make this subject an important one to every man and woman, boy and girl alive today.

The background of our text is important. It might seem to the casual reader that Paul, the apostle, was writing to the Philippian believers from a comfortable chair in a luxury suite in some five-star hotel. But the truth is that he was writing from a cold, dark prison in Rome. In spite of this, his tone was comforting and encouraging. This shows us that in the cold, dark places of our lives, God will be with us, and we can have His joy, just as Paul did.

Paul was determined to raise the bar, to improve the attitude of the Philippian believers. He said: *"The things which you learned and received and heard and saw in me, these do, and [then] the peace of God will be with you"* (Philippians 4:9).

How could a man who was imprisoned speak with such liberty? This proves that it's not our circumstances that determine our success, but our state of mind. How can we each develop similar attitudes?

## REJOICE IN THE PRESENCE OF THE LORD

If you're going to develop a right attitude (and I'm not talking about the fake, or phony, attitude, or fake, or phony, persona that we sometimes display just to impress people), you need to learn to rejoice in God. As I noted before, many of us in the body of Christ have been taught that it's all about doing, but actually it's all about being. You will never be able to do what you're supposed to do until you become who you are supposed to be. You will never be able to do what you are supposed to do until you learn who you are and have your attitude about life changed.

The very first thing we should do to move toward victory in our lives is to learn to rejoice in God. What did Paul say? *"Rejoice in the Lord always"* (Verse 4). But is that possible? How can we *"always"* be rejoicing when we're going through trials at work and at home? We're dealing with some two-faced people, and that's never easy.

But we're not called to rejoice in our troubles, in our negative circumstances, or in the people around us. We are called to rejoice *"in the Lord."*

That's very different. He never changes, and He's always by our side. And knowing these truths can change everything about our day. No wonder Paul could rejoice even in prison!

"But how can we be so sure of the Lord's presence with us?" some might ask. I would answer this way: "Because He said so. That's why." Indeed, His Word declares:

*He Himself has said, "I will never leave you nor forsake you." So we may boldly say: "The Lord is my helper; I will not fear. What can man do to me?"*

Hebrews 13:5-6

*And lo, I am with you always, even to the end of the age.*

Matthew 28:20

I can't say for sure what you've gone through this particular week, but I can imagine because I know what the enemy wants to accomplish in your life. He's always there, intent upon stealing your joy. He knows the truth of the Scriptures that declare:

*The joy of the Lord is your strength.*

Nehemiah 8:10

Since joy is your strength, the devil knows that if he can steal your joy, he will eventually have all of you. That's why the apostle Paul encouraged us all to rejoice in the Lord, and to do it *"always."* Then he repeated it: *"Again I will say, rejoice!"*

The joy of the Lord in your life will make you a thermostat, not a thermometer. What do I mean by that? A thermometer registers conditions, telling you what the current temperature is, but a thermostat does much more. It actually controls the level of the temperature in a given space. That's what must happen in your life.

You cannot allow the circumstances around you to hinder your joy. You can be in trouble without allowing trouble to be in you. Understanding who you are in God will cause your joy to remain constant.

I'm not talking here about being happy. Happiness is based on what's happening around you. Your happenings determine your happiness, but happenings should have nothing at all to do with your joy. Absolutely crazy things can be happening around you, and your joy can remain insulated from them all.

God is more than just a figment of your imagination. He is real, and He is with you everywhere you go. Even when you're in the valley, you can still have joy. If God is with you, you can have daily victory. You may well be in a valley, but God will guide you through every dark situation and bring you out.

A knowledge that the Lord is always with you becomes a monitor for your behavior, a watchdog for your lifestyle. We might be able to fool each other, but we can't fool God. We can hide from one another, but there's no place to hide from God. He's everywhere. Recognizing that fact and beginning to rejoice in His presence will do wonders for your attitude.

God is present, even when you can't feel Him. He's present, even when you can't see Him. As the prophet Elijah learned, He's not always in the rushing, mighty wind. Sometimes He's in the *"still small voice"* (1 Kings 19:12).

God is not only with you, but He is orchestrating the events of your life so that you will learn to trust Him and depend on Him. Can you imagine what it would be like to go through what you've been going through without having the Lord on your side? Some of you who are reading this book are only here because the Lord has been with you every step of the way. Rejoice in the Lord.

The prophet Habakkuk knew what it was to rejoice in the Lord in difficult times:

> *Though the fig tree may not blossom, nor fruit be on the vines, though the labor of the olive may fail, and the fields yield no food: though the flock be cut off from the fold, and there be no herd in the stalls—yet I will rejoice in the Lord, I will joy in the God of my salvation.*

> Habakkuk 3:17-18

Joy has nothing to do with what's happening on the outside, what's going on in your neighborhood, or what might be lacking on your table or in your garage. None of these things produce joy. A person might be driving a Mercedes and still not have joy. Some can live in a nice split-level home and still not have joy.

In the same way, the absence of these things must not be allowed to rob us of joy. When you come to understand the joy of the Lord, you can stand at the bus stop in the rain and still have joy in your heart. You can wear a borrowed T-shirt and still have joy. You can know that where you are right now is not where you will always stay. You're just in between buses. You're in transition to greater things. Joy is never based on what's happening around you. Joy is not in what you go through, but in how you view what you're going through. Attitude is everything.

*The secret to developing a right attitude is to rejoice in His presence.*

One of our members in New Orleans asked me to pray with her that she would get a house she had bid on. When someone else won the bid, she was very sad and called me.

"Well, Girl, you'd better praise God," I said.

"No, Bishop," she protested. "You didn't understand what I said."

"Oh, but I did understand what you said," I insisted.

I could sense that she was puzzled. "Are you in the will of God?" I asked.

"I am," she answered.

"Then you need to rejoice with me, because if you didn't get that house it's because God has a better house for you, one with a lower interest rate." That seemed to help her understand that God had not forgotten her.

When we know who we are, we cannot allow bad news to be bad news to us. For instance, when someone brings me what seems like bad news, I rejoice. I can do this because I know that when the Lord shuts one door it's because He's about to open a bigger and better one.

It's time to rejoice in the Lord. You've been stressing yourself out over circumstances that God has allowed for some good reason. The secret to developing a right attitude is to rejoice in His presence. That shows that you trust what He's doing in your life.

## LEARN TO RELY ON THE POWER OF THE LORD

Rejoicing in the presence of the Lord is just the beginning. You must learn to rely on His power. The Scriptures admonish us: *"Be anxious for nothing"* (Philippians 4:6). This word *anxious* means "careful, full of anxiety, tense, rigid." In our common everyday vernacular, we would say, "He's 'all bent out of shape.'" And we get "all bent out of shape" over things we can do absolutely nothing about. We lose sleep over problems that we expect to face the next day. Paul said: *"Be anxious for nothing, but in everything by prayer and supplication, with thanksgiving, let your requests be made known to God"* (Philippians 4:6). It's all about being, not doing. Because you are His child, you can ask Him for what you need and know that He will supply it.

Here's a deep thought: If you have a problem, tell the Lord about it. Here's another deep thought: Once you've told the Lord about it, stop worrying about it. Trust Him to take care of it.

Some of us give things to the Lord, only to take them right back again. That's what we call an Indian giver. God's Word says:

*Casting all your care upon Him, for He cares for you.*

1 Peter 5:7

So what are we worrying about? Why are we constantly fretting about this or that? Worry is one of the most damaging of all emotions. It can literally kill you.

This word *worry* comes from a Greek root that means "to be pulled apart," and that's exactly what worry does to you. It pulls you apart, causing you to live between hope and fear. You have an idea that things might get better, but you're afraid they won't. So you're pulled back and forth by those two opposing views.

In His Sermon on the Mount, Jesus taught us that worry is useless. It is misused or abused imagination, and, as such, it is insulting to God. When you worry, you're saying that you're not sure that God can handle your problem. And you go back and forth. You know that He has the power to do it, and yet you're not sure that He will. Nothing could be more insulting to Him!

Worry is like a rocking chair. It gives you something to do, but it gets you nowhere. It seems that worry is all that some people accomplish in life, and that is very sad.

There they are ... . They're rocking. They're occupied, but with what? And to what end? They're not gaining any ground. They're not accomplishing anything in life. Worry is very damaging to the mind, and it's also a waste of time and effort.

Behavioral psychologists teach us that forty percent of what we worry about never happens, so we have no reason to worry about it. Thirty percent of what we worry about has already happened, so no amount of worry can change it. Twelve percent of our worries are about our health, and worry only makes any real health problem worse. Ten percent of what we worry about relates to inconsequential matters, unworthy of any serious consideration. That leaves only eight percent of our worries that are about anything that should ever be considered as worthy of worry.

Among the eight percent of our worries that are about things worth worrying about, only half are about something we can do anything about. That leaves only four percent of our worries that are worthy of consideration, and since Christians commit their lives to God and trust Him for His best, we should not even worry about that four percent.

Worrying only pulls tomorrow's clouds over today's sunshine, and, in the process, it does nothing to help you get ready for what you will face in the future. Still, worry has become, for many, a lifestyle. Why?

When you bring tomorrow's trouble into today, you overload today, and worry is the interest you constantly pay on borrowed trouble. When tomorrow finally arrives, you will be so out of breath and emotionally overwrought that you won't be able to deal with the day effectively.

When you overload today, then you're mentally exhausted before you even get to tomorrow. Worry about nothing, and pray about everything. That's the very best policy.

Some people foolishly decide that they shouldn't "bother" God with their "little" problems. They only take the "big" ones to Him. But to God, what is "big" and what is "little"? What problem could possibly intimidate Him? Is there anything that He's afraid to tackle? What might be a "big" problem to you might not be "big" to God at all.

At the same time, nothing is too small for God's concern. Bring Him everything. Cast every care upon Him. Present every situation to Him. Rejoice in the presence of the Lord, and then learn to rely on His power.

## REFLECT ON THE PROVISION OF THE LORD

When problems arise in our lives, many of us seem to have spiritual amnesia, for we forget what God has done for us in the past. Didn't the Lord come through for you the last time you had a problem? Didn't He make a way for you the last time you had a great need? Each time a need arises, begin to reflect on the provision of the Lord in the past. As Paul wrote, *"Be anxious for nothing, but in everything by prayer and supplication, with thanksgiving, let your requests be made known to God"* (Philippians 4:6).

"*With thanksgiving...*" That's the key. Thanksgiving is the highest expression of faith. We can say to the Lord, "I don't understand what is happening in my life, but I thank You because I'm confident that

*Thanksgiving is* You're working out Your plan for me just as You have in the past. Lord, the answer to my prayers has not yet been

*the highest* manifested, but I thank You because I know that if You said You would do it, You will. You've always been faith-

*expression* ful in the past."

When I think back on what I've already been

*of faith.* through (that should have wiped me out, but didn't), I know that I have to preface any new requests to the Lord with a thank-you. Thanking Him for what He's already done encourages my faith that He will now do what I need Him to do.

Dr. C.A.W. Clark, a preacher who sowed into the lives of many of us, often said, "When you T-H-I-N-K, you can't help but T-H-A-N-K." I dare you to review in your mind some of the things God has brought you and your family through, and I promise you that in the process your current problems will diminish in importance.

That wasn't just luck that got you through those things. You didn't have the resources to get out of those situations. In the natural, things looked very bad for you, but you cried out to God, and, in the end, He came through for you. He may not have acted when you wanted Him to, but in His own perfect timing He took care of the situation. He's always right on time.

Sometimes God will allow a situation in our lives to go from bad to worse just to show us how much power He has. This was true in the case of Lazarus, Jesus' friend.

At first, Jesus heard that Lazarus was sick. With that, the disciples expected Him to drop everything and rush off to Bethany. He didn't do that. He remained where He was for several more days.

Had Jesus not heard the news correctly? Did He not know that His friend Lazarus was seriously ill? Did He not realize that the family had expected Him to come quickly when He received the initial report of serious illness? Oh, He knew all right. But He had another plan—a greater plan.

56

After several days, word came that Lazarus had died, and Jesus decided that it was now time to go to Bethany. This left the disciples totally perplexed. Why had Jesus not gone in time to heal His friend?

But we can trust in the goodness of the Lord. He knows our situation, and He knows what's best for us. If He delays in acting on our behalf, it's because He has something better in mind for us. He not only wanted to heal Lazarus; He wanted to raise Him from the dead. So just praise the Lord in your situation, for thanksgiving is a high expression of faith.

The psalmist declared:

*Blessed be the Lord, Who daily loads us with benefits.*

Psalm 68:19

Our God does things for us *"daily,"* so we can trust Him with every problem. He opens doors for us on the job, in our home, and in our day-to-day affairs. When you go to your doctor, and he gives you a clean bill of health, you can know that it's not just because you've eaten the right foods and drunk the right amount of water. That helps, but your health is also the grace of God in action. He *"daily loads us with benefits."*

The psalmist went on to identify our Benefactor more fully:

*The God of our salvation! Selah.*

Psalm 68:19

This word *selah* means to pause and think about it, to ponder over it. God is good, and His goodness is extended to us on a daily basis. That's worth pondering.

Stop complaining about the events of the day, and start blessing God for what He did for you yesterday. Have you forgotten how He watched over you last night? Have you forgotten to thank Him for saving your life when you fell asleep at the wheel and were about to run off the road? Have you thanked Him that He caused the drunk driver who passed you on the interstate to avoid hitting you? He has brought you through many dangers, and He will bring you through many more.

I have noticed in our church services that unthankful people are also unhappy people. They sit in their seats disgusted because someone else is praising God. "They don't have to be doing all that," they say to themselves and others. "They're much too loud. I'm just not like that. I'm grateful, but I'm not emotional about it." But when you realize what God has done, how can you not become emotional about it?

Raising my hands to praise God doesn't mean that I don't have any problems. It means that I'm surrendering my all to the Problem-Solver. I praise Him because I know that when I send up praises, He sends down blessings. I'm not trying to get any person's attention. I want God's attention. What the Lord has done for me and all the things He's already brought me through compel me to seek Him more.

Thankful people have smiles on their faces, not necessarily because they have more money in their pockets, but because they know the Source of all things. A smile on your face means that you have hope in your heart and faith for your future.

You may not have the best life has to offer, but if you'll thank God for what you do have, He will give you more. Your house may not be a mansion, but at least you have a house. That's more than many have. Your car may not be the latest model, but it's getting you to where you need to go. The food on your table may not be filet mignon, but at least you have something to eat. So be thankful.

Remember, again, that Paul was in prison when he wrote all of this. There in that terrible place, he had to keep a healthy attitude. He had to rejoice in the presence of the Lord, he had to learn to rely on the power of the Lord, and he had to reflect on the faithful provision of the Lord. And if he could do that in a prison as he awaited his fate, surely we can do it in the circumstances of our lives today in the twenty-first century.

Far too many Christians just go through the motions of worship. They sing when others sing and pray when others pray, but there's no real power, no real glory. Even in church, they seem to be there only in body. Their mind is somewhere else entirely. The devil loves that. He doesn't want us to open our hearts and receive a new attitude. He knows that a "right" attitude will attract the "right" people to us, so that we can be blessed. As long as he can keep us with a bad attitude, he can keep from us the very people who are destined to bless us. And don't be guilty of spending time around people who are negative.

Rejoice in the presence of the Lord, rely on the power of the Lord, reflect on the provision of the Lord, and then rest in the peace of the Lord.

## REST IN THE PEACE OF THE LORD

Next, Paul gave the final piece of the puzzle. We must rest in the peace of the Lord. Peace and the rest it brings is what I declare over your life this very day. Your mind has been going much too fast. You haven't even been able to rest as you sleep. Your mind has been bombarded with thoughts, not only all day long, but also all night long.

As we have seen, many of us are worried about things that will never happen. It may be that your mind is overloaded with worry, your concentration is at the breaking point, and your nerves are shot. As a result, your blood pressure is up, and your stomach often feels upset. Worry affects your nervous system, and that affects every other part of your being.

Worry eventually affects your digestive tract, but it can also cause you not to enjoy what you eat. You may feel such a lump in your throat that it's difficult for you to enjoy a good meal. It's time to stop worrying and to rest in the peace of the Lord.

When God saved you, He put you on the winning track in life. When He redeemed you, He not only redeemed you from past failure, but He also made you a winner. He didn't save your soul, only to see you defeated. What glory would He have in that? He saved you to make you a conqueror. So get winning on your mind. Change your perspective on life. Change your attitude today.

Start saying to yourself, "I'm coming out of this, and when I come out, I'm coming out with victory. I will continue to raise my hands and praise God because I know He hasn't brought me this far just to leave me now. Don't ask me how He's going to do it. I don't know how He's going to do it. I didn't know how He was going to do it the last time, but He did it anyway. And I know He'll do it again."

Let your spirit and mind be at rest. Let the peace of God flood your soul today.

Peace is not the subtraction of problems; peace is the addition of power to handle those problems. It's not that you won't have any more problems, but you'll have power to handle every problem that comes your way.

The peace you need today is the *"peace that passes all understanding."* And you don't "keep" this peace; this peace "keeps" you. You can't get this kind of peace from a bottle or a syringe. You can't get this kind of peace out of a book, and you can't get it by sitting on a psychoanalyst's couch. This is the peace Isaiah foretold:

*You will keep him in perfect peace, whose mind is stayed on You.*

Isaiah 26:3

Begin to reflect more on the purpose of God in all that you experience, and thus choose your thoughts just as you do your friends. When Satan sends a thought your way, and you know that it's not from God, send it back where it came from. When the devil says that you'll never get out of this particular situation, reject that thought. When he says that your sickness will only get worse, tell him that he's a liar. Become more selective about what you choose to let rest in your mind.

Even though Paul was in prison, he refused to be imprisoned in his mind and spirit. His body was bound, but His spirit was free. And God is setting you free right now. Relax in His arms, and let Him do it today. You've been held down by a job, a boss, a friend, a neighbor, or a neighborhood. That old mind-set has been powerful and it controlled you, but today it is being broken. Be free in your mind so that you can develop the "right" kind of attitude.

Why would you continue to worry? Jesus said:

*Therefore do not worry about tomorrow, for tomorrow will worry about its own things. Sufficient for the day is its own trouble.*

Matthew 6:34

Worrying doesn't help anything. Jesus asked:

*Which of you by worrying can add one cubit to his stature?*

Matthew 6:27

You can't change it, so why worry about it? Trust in the Lord and develop a positive attitude. Develop the "right" attitude, the attitude for righteous living.

Let go of the things that have held you back. Let go of the things that have hindered you. Your mind has insisted, "This is the way I am; and this is the way I will always be. Good things will never happen for me." But we know that the devil is a liar. Reject his lies today. Instead, rejoice in the Lord, and do it *"always"*!

This word will change your life if you let it. Worship God, and things will get better for you. Give Him the praise due to His name, and your situation will improve. He will always come through for you.

If you can develop "right" attitudes about every aspect, you will be well on your way to *Doing "Right" in a Wrong World.*

# CHAPTER 7

# What's "Right" for You
# as a Believer?

*Even so, every good tree bears good fruit, but a bad tree bears bad fruit. A good tree cannot bear bad fruit, nor can a bad tree bear good fruit. Every tree that does not bear good fruit is cut down and thrown into the fire.*

Matthew 7:17-19

If we are to develop a "right" attitude and "right" thinking, there are certain ideas that we must embrace. In this chapter, I want to name twenty things that need to become part of your thinking. You need to start meditating on these things, and then you need to start implementing them in your daily life. They are part of God's will for you and your future.

The order in which I have chosen to list these twenty attributes here has no particular significance. It's a simple alphabetical order. You may wish to reorder these subjects by personal preference or in the order of importance to your own personal life. For instance, you may want to list first the things you know are lacking in you. Whatever the case, I want these twenty words to become part of your everyday vocabulary, part of your everyday consciousness, and part of your everyday habits.

## NEEDED: MATURITY

Why is this so important? If you would pause and take notice of the words coming out of the mouth of the average Christian today, you would find these particular words strangely missing. These are words that we now hear very seldom, if at all, but they are words that should be spoken more and more in the days ahead. God wills it to be so, and He will bless those who chose to live "right."

When Paul spoke of having been a child, and, of having had childish ways of thinking, understanding and speaking, he was referring to the great change that had come over his life. At some dramatic point, his thinking had changed, his attitudes had changed, his way of talking had changed, and his way of living had changed. He had become a changed man. Far too often the thinking of our modern Christians is very elementary, very childish. It's time to grow up and to act like we're grown up.

Adults, because of experience, look beyond an act and see the consequences. Children usually can't do that because their experience is too limited. You may be saved, and you may love God, but do you still have childish ways of thinking and acting that are holding you back?

Are you an adult? Meaning, do you have understanding? Or are you still a child? When things don't go your way, do you sit in the middle of the floor and have a temper tantrum? Lots of adults still do that.

Husbands and wives get angry at each other, and then they walk around in the same house without speaking to each other. That's childish.

When it comes time for bed, they each face the other way and try to make sure that their feet don't touch. That's childish.

Some get so angry that they break furniture and lamps they haven't even finished paying for yet. When that happens, they then have to make monthly payments on something they can't even enjoy. That's childish.

It's time for us to act our age. We all have done and continue to do some childish things, but God is calling for maturity.

Here, then, are twenty things that must become a part of your daily life, part of your thinking, and part of your way of speaking. If these words are not part of your consciousness, they will never filter over into your lifestyle.

# ACHIEVEMENT

Relatively few people are talking about achievement these days, and when you're not reaching for something, you'll settle for anything. If you don't know where you're going, you'll never know when you have arrived or even if you have arrived. How can you move toward some achievement in life if that word is not yet a part of your thinking and your vocabulary?

What does the word *achievement* mean? It means "to accomplish, to win, to attain, to do successfully." That's what God wants for you. Whatever it is that He has placed in your heart to do, He has equipped you by the Spirit to complete it successfully. You are destined for achievement in life, and it's time to begin reaching your God-given goals.

Start by declaring, "I am a winner," and then start acting like a winner. Prepare yourself for the greater things that God wants to send your way in the days ahead, because you will never attain to something that you are incapable of maintaining. God will never give you something you cannot handle.

We often quote the scriptural promise that God will give us the desires of our hearts:

> *Delight yourself also in the Lord, and He shall give you the desires of your heart.*
>
> Psalm 37:4

This is a very powerful promise, and we all love to claim it, but this promise comes to us only when we have grown up enough to handle the desires God has placed in our hearts, when our desires have become God's desires. He wants you to have many accomplishments in life. Start going after them today.

# COMPASSION

Far too many Christian never utter this important word *compassion* in their daily conversation, and that has to change. If the word *compassion* never comes out of your mouth, it must mean that it's not in your heart. And that's serious. Jesus said:

> *A good man out of the good treasure of his heart brings forth good; and an evil man out of the evil treasure of his heart brings forth evil. For out of the abundance of the heart his mouth speaks.*
>
> Luke 6:45

What's in you will come out, and if compassion is not present, you're in trouble.

Some people talk about themselves all the time, and when you hear them talking, it's easy to know what's in their heart. They're stuck on themselves.

When you have compassion you begin to think of others, because the word *compassion* means "pity with the desire to help," and unless and until you have genuine compassion in your heart, you can't help the many people who cross your path every day.

God is bringing people into our lives, just as He did into the life of His Son Jesus while He was on earth as a man, and God is doing this for the same reason He brought people into contact with Jesus—so that they can be changed. Therefore we must begin to look upon others as Jesus did.

When Jesus looked at a multitude, He saw them as *"sheep not having a shepherd"*:

> *And Jesus, when He came out, saw a great multitude and was moved with compassion for them, because they were like sheep not having a shepherd. So He began to teach them many things.*
>
> Mark 6:34

To Jesus, these were scattered lambs, and He felt compassion for them and helped them. And because we're Christians, followers of Christ, His representatives in the earth, God causes people who need a helping hand to cross our paths. He doesn't do this so that we can criticize them and point out the wrong choices they've made in life. He does it so that we can demonstrate His love to them, and in this way, He can change their lives.

When people in need come to you, what do you feel? Are you moved with disgust and disdain? Or do you feel the genuine compassion of the Lord toward them?

The people God is sending your way quite possibly have never before been shown compassion, and He is calling upon you to be the person who first offers them this grace. Why do it? Well, if you need a selfish motive, there is one. When this person you're helping today rises to the top, they will remember you and bless you. So be compassionate—for Jesus' sake, and also for the sake of your own future.

When you see someone in need, it's not enough just to stand at a distance and pray for them. If God has allowed you to see their need, then you can meet it, and He is calling you to do it.

Sometimes we resent people who want to draw from us, but you're constantly drawing from God, so you should be able to support the fact that others need to draw from you. Jesus said:

*Heal the sick, cleanse the lepers, raise the dead, cast out demons. Freely you have received, freely give.*

Matthew 10:8

If you're bothered by the needy, check your heart today. You may need more of the compassion of Christ.

There're not nearly enough truly compassionate Christians in the world today. Churchgoers can sometimes be among the most unforgiving people in the world. They are very partial in their good treatment to some and not to others, and this is not pleasing to God. He *"shows no partiality"* (Acts 10:34), and He has called us to be like Him.

Strive to minister the compassion of Christ to everyone around you, and your life will be enriched in the process. Those who are up and care nothing for those who are down will eventually join them. Personally, I'm not nearly as judgmental as I used to be, and I'm much more patient with those who are down now. I've come to understand that we're all struggling against the flesh.

God has been very patient with me, so how can I not be patient with others? God has been very forgiving to me, so how can I not be forgiving of my brothers?

"But that person didn't keep his word," we sometimes protest.

No, and you didn't keep your word either, but God forgave you nevertheless.

As Christ has been compassionate to you, be compassionate toward others.

## COURAGE

*Courage* is "a quality of spirit that enables one to face danger," and we all need more of it. Courage gives you another needed attribute—tenacity. In the midst of serious spiritual warfare, courage and tenacity cause you to refuse to back down.

Instead, you develop an attitude that says, "Devil, bring on whatever you want to; I'm ready for you. If God has allowed this to come to my life, it must be because He knows I can handle it. And, as bad as things may seem, I know that if I continue to trust God, He will make a way for me somehow."

Many of us, when trouble shows up, tuck our tail between our legs and run like a scared puppy dog. But when we're bound by fear God cannot use us or move us into a place of excellence in His kingdom. His promise is this:

> *For God has not given us a spirit of fear, but of power and of love and of a sound mind.*
>
> 2 Timothy 1:7

This phrase *a spirit of fear* refers to "timidity, cowardice." Such a spirit is not of God. He has not called us to be timid, but to be bold.

The words *courage, courageous,* and *courageously* are found throughout the Bible. Joshua urged the people under his charge to *"be very courageous"* (Joshua 1:7 and 23:6), and we still need that admonition today. How can God take us to the level He wants if we're afraid to go there?

This walk with God requires the participation of warriors, not wimps. God is calling you to be courageous today. Courage will not only enable you to stand in the face of danger; it will enable you to maintain a good spirit as you do so.

Say to yourself every morning, "I don't know what might come my way today, but I know that the Lord is with me, and with His help I can handle whatever comes. Even in moments of danger, I trust Him." And then go out to face the day with courage and tenacity.

## CREATIVITY

God is the Creator, and He longs to place creativity of many kinds into His children. Sadly, most of us settle for mediocrity and a life of very little creativity.

Our city of New Orleans is not called "The Big Easy" for nothing. There's a spirit that hovers over our city and tries to trap everyone in it in a state of "normality." Far too many of our New Orlean citizens are satisfied with very little in life. As a pastor in this city, I feel compelled to challenge my people to ever higher heights. I have to say to them periodically, "You have too much potential to live such a limited life." But this is also true of people all over the world.

In many respects, this is probably true in your life as well. Many ideas flood you on the inside, but because you're hesitant to step out of the box, and because you would much rather be popular than peculiar, there isn't much God can do for you. If you prefer to fit in than to stand out, His hands are tied.

*Creativity is "having the power or the ability to create, to cause to come to existence."*

God is trying to bring creativity to your life, and if you'll accept it, you can begin to enjoy life as you never have before. You're existing, but are you really living? It's time to break forth into a whole new realm of living.

*Creativity* is "having the power or the ability to create, to cause to come to existence." Many things are lying dormant and unclaimed in your life because you've not yet tapped into the creativity God has gifted you with. There are, for instance, inventions within you just waiting to be released.

Everything that we have and enjoy in our homes and offices and places of business today, all of our modern inventions, existed first in the mind of someone. Someone was gifted with creativity, and the many apparatuses you use are the result. Why not let God make you the one to be creative?

Who should be more creative than the very sons and daughters of God, the Creator of all things? We just need to recognize what's already in us and learn how to use it.

Creativity is not a question of natural intelligence. God has gifted us all with some special talent. We just need to have it discovered and then put to work. It's already there. What's your special unique ability?

There's something on the inside of you that you need to let come out. What's your dream, your special goal in life? Is there a God-inspired ambition in your soul, an idea that consumes you? If you continue to smother it, God will have no choice but to use someone else.

When I was about ten or eleven years old, my only brother, whom we have always called Kippie, said something that I never forgot. We were always building something with our hands, especially model cars. We loved cars. One day

Kippie said, "Someday I'm going to come up with an invention that will prevent many accidents. It will be a third brake light in the center of the back window of a car, and it will make it easier for the cars behind to see because it will be at eye level."

That was in 1976, and just a few years later, a law was passed requiring such a light in all new cars on the road. Today, this feature is standard on every new car, and many accidents have been prevented in the intervening years through its use.

Someone made millions of dollars from that idea, but my brother had it years before it became popular. He just didn't do anything with the idea.

What's in you? God has not made you like everyone else. On the inside of you are ideas that could transform the world and aid society in every country. You just need to get them out.

How do you begin? All you have to do is get out of the boat, and the rest will take care of itself. If you will just step out, God will back you.

"What if you fail?" Satan will taunt.

Answer him, "What if I don't fail?"

Several years ago, the Lord told me to go to the coastal town of Houma, Louisiana. There were people there, He said, who needed and wanted the Gospel, and I should establish a church there.

But, oh, how the devil fought me over that idea! "What if you go there, and it doesn't work?" he taunted.

But I knew that God had spoken. I went to Houma and preached, and today our church there is the fastest growing church in the area.

Next, the Lord told me to do the same thing in Hammond, Louisiana, on the other side of Lake Ponchartrain. "You're really about to 'mess up' this time!" the devil taunted me. "What will you do if it doesn't work?"

But, again, I knew that God was in it. I obeyed, and it worked.

Next, the Lord spoke to me to start a work in Baton Rouge, our capital city. That seemed like a stretch. There were many churches already in the city. Why did I need to start another one? The devil fought it, but I persisted, and our church in the capital city is growing and prospering today.

When we were still in a small location here in New Orleans, the Lord spoke to me to begin having two services each Sunday morning. "What if no one comes to the second service?" Satan taunted.

"What if someone does?" I answered.

The second service proved so successful that later we extended it to three morning services, and then to four and then to five services each Sunday. We never know what God will do until we take the risk to try something.

There's creativity within you today. God has given you the ability to bring forth something worthwhile and useful, to cause it to come to existence.

Your brain is the exact same size as that of the man who came up with an invention that earned him millions of dollars. Start putting your God-given creativity to work, and see what God will do for you.

## FAITH

As Christians, we know the word *faith*, and we sometimes use it, but too often the reality of it has not yet become a part of us. This must change. *Faith* is "belief without need of certain proof, to have confidence in or dependence on a person or thing as being trustworthy." God is trying to increase our spiritual potential, and that requires more faith on our part.

Do you have confidence in the Lord? Can you know that even though you're not sure how it will happen, He will somehow make a way? As I often say, He may not come when you want Him to, but He will always be on time. Just when you need Him the most, He'll be there.

Sometimes God will remove the very things and the very people who make up your support system so that you can learn to trust Him more. In those moments, your faith is on trial. When this happens, you must hold steady. You cannot afford to be double-minded. That is, you can't trust God one moment and begin to doubt Him the next. The apostle James wrote:

*Let him ask in faith, with no doubting, for he who doubts is like a wave of the sea driven and tossed by the wind. For let not that man suppose that he will receive anything from the Lord; he is a double-minded man, unstable in all his ways.*

James 1:6-8

When you are double-minded, it throws everything off. Either you're going to trust God and believe Him, or you're not. There is no in-between.

71

God has proven that He is trustworthy again and again, and therefore you should have no problem having confidence in Him and depending on Him.

Many times, when we're rebuking something that has come into our lives, we are actually rebuking God. He permitted that thing to happen so that we would trust Him more. And when we suddenly find ourselves stripped of resources, we can know that God is still in control. He is Jehovah Jireh, the Lord who will provide, and you can trust Him to provide for your particular needs.

Sometimes God will allow you to get a terrible report from your doctor just so that He can prove to you that He's still the Healer (Jehovah Raphe, the Lord who heals). Trust Him to heal you.

Stop cursing your crisis, because it may be centered on Christ. Instead, release faith in your life for things to be changed.

Faith must become more than just a part of your vocabulary. Let it be part of your thinking and part of your acting. Wake up every morning exercising the principles of faith. Stop playing it safe, and don't be impatient.

In our modern world, so much is available to us instantly that we now want instant answers, and if God doesn't answer us right now, we lose patience. But don't be guilty of entertaining a spirit of shortsightedness. God will answer in His time. So just trust Him.

Most of us have this problem to one degree or another. All we can see is where we are right now. We must learn to see ahead, and many of these things can be seen only in the Spirit.

You must learn to say, "It has not yet been manifested, but it's mine. It has not yet been manifested, but I know it's real." And when your faith rises to the point that you begin to talk and act like the thing you so desperately need is already yours, then it becomes yours.

By this, you are doing what the Scriptures advise, *"calling things which be not as though they were"* (KJV):

*(As it is written, "I have made you a father of many nations") in the presence of Him whom he believed—God, who gives life to the dead and calls those things which do not exist as though they did.*

Romans 4:17

Begin to confess God's promise that you will be the head and not the tail, that you will be above and not beneath, that you will be blessed in the city and blessed in the fields, blessed coming in and blessed going out. Your children will be blessed, your car will be blessed, and your house will be blessed. Everything associated with you will be blessed.

Let faith become an integral part of you, and when God does things to test you, trust Him that He knows what He's doing and has your best interests at heart.

Are you walking by faith?

*For we walk by faith, not by sight.*

2 Corinthians 5:7

Are you living by faith?

*For therein is the righteousness of God revealed from faith to faith: as it is written, The just shall live by faith.*

Romans 1:17

Some of us want to see God's blessings so badly, and we're walking with Him. But He is trying to challenge us to greater things. He is saying to us, "How about if you do something you've never done to get something you've never had?" Obeying these challenging words will change your life.

As your thinking changes in this regard, your speech will begin to change, and that will strike terror in the heart of the enemy. He knows what the Scriptures declare:

*Death and life are in the power of the tongue, and those who love it will eat its fruit.*

Proverbs 18:21

The enemy knows that once you learn the principles of positive confession and begin to speak out the truths of God, you will be able to shake his kingdom. So speak it, and you will see it come to pass.

But if all you speak is the problem, then that's all you'll get. This may not make sense to some, but then faith doesn't make sense. Faith is faith, and sense is sense. If something starts making sense, then it's no longer faith at work. Stop trying to make sense of it, and start declaring it to be so.

If you're controlled by your senses—what you see, what you hear, what you feel, what you taste, and what you smell—you can't live and walk by faith. Let faith be your motivation today and every day.

## HEALTH

Another word that will enhance your vocabulary and your consciousness of God's will for your life is the word *health*. Too many of us are not paying enough attention to our health.

*Health* means "to be free from defect or disease," and that's God's will for you. How can you love God and not be health conscious? How can you love Him and not take care of yourself?

*God wants to give you longevity, but you're trying to kill yourself with what you eat.*

It's time that we stopped living in the fast lane. Too many are sleeping, but not really resting. Too many are not eating right and not drinking the right amount of water. If you don't pay attention to your health, who will? If you allow yourself to develop terrible eating habits, then shame on you.

People are so busy today that they just grab whatever they can on the move, and they're putting all the wrong things into their stomachs. Then, when they get a bad report from their doctor, the first thing they want to do is start rebuking the devil. But you're the one who needs to be rebuked. Your body is the temple of God. He has chosen to take up residence within you, and yet you persist in defiling His temple.

Some of us wonder why we can no longer go up a flight of steps without getting out of breath, but the truth is that we take better care of our automobiles than we do of our own bodies. You would never put a quart of oil in your radiator (well, maybe some would, but if you know how your engine works, you would never do that). And yet there are many harmful things that we're ingesting into our system. This is threatening our future.

God wants to give you longevity, but you're trying to kill yourself with what you eat. As a result, many Christians are dying young, and this should not happen.

"Exercise? What's that?" It doesn't even cross our minds on many busy days. We don't have time for it, and we don't want to have time for it.

Eating whatever you want and failing to get enough exercise might be considered by some to be part of "the good life," but God wants us to live "right." This means eating what is good for us and doing what will prolong our lives and give us the health to do God's will and enjoy doing it.

Healthy people feel better in general. They have sharper minds. They're more pleasant to deal with. They have a more positive attitude toward life. It's time to do whatever is necessary to improve your health.

Unfortunately, most of us in the black community never think of health-related issues until it's too late, until we receive a diagnosis of some serious illness from our doctor. But prevention is always better than a cure. Don't wait until you're seriously ill to start eating right and treating your body right.

Do you have a good variety of fruits in your home? Many don't. But they do have candy bars and snack foods. Recently I was buying a magazine in an airport shop and saw a sight I will never forget. A lady who was very overweight was buying two Snickers bars and a Diet Coke. Something is very wrong with that picture, don't you think?

God wants you to have health, but in order for that to happen, you're going to have to become more health conscious. If you want to be around for a long time, you're going to have to take better care of yourself. That body of yours, as much as you might not like it, is the only one you'll ever have, so get used to it and start taking better care of it.

You can abuse a car and eventually trade it in on another one, but those feet you have are the only feet you'll ever have. You'd better take better care of your feet. If they go bad, you won't have any spare to replace them.

Realize how important health is to your future and make whatever changes are necessary today to maintain a sound body.

## HONESTY

Sadly, it is becoming increasingly difficult to find people of honesty in our modern society. Most of us have been misused and abused by people who prey upon the innocent with their lies. Abusive people seem to be everywhere, and we sometimes wonder which way to turn. Is everyone dishonest and lacking in integrity and character? Who can we trust?

As we noted previously, it seems many of the people we come in contact with are intent on getting something from us, and the moment we have nothing more to give to them, they move on to someone else. That's just a fact of life today, and we have to learn to deal with it. Most people are not honest. That's a fact of modern life.

This word *honesty* means "fairness, straightforwardness, integrity, upright-ness of character." Straightforwardness is something we don't see much of today in relationships, including friendships, marriages, and business relation-ships. It's time for honesty, honesty with God and honesty with one another.

It's time to tell the truth, or as we say these days, to "tell it like it is." You need honesty from the people with whom you are in relationship, and they need honesty from you. And if there is no honesty in the relationship, you need to get other relationships.

You don't need people around you who sugarcoat the truth. When you're acting like a fool, someone needs to tell you that you're acting like a fool. And just as you need honest friends around you, be an honest friend to others. Don't say one thing to people's faces and another thing behind their backs. Speak the truth. Be honest. Be a person of integrity. Jesus said:

*Blessed are the pure in heart, for they shall see God.*

Matthew 5:8

The truth is that we love to be lied to. Admit it, and change today so that you can be blessed. God wants to add honesty to your character, a desire to hear truth and to speak truth.

The worst thing about the climate of dishonesty that prevails in our times is that many don't see anything wrong with it. That is truly a tragedy.

God wants to put people in our lives to whom we can minister, but He's having a hard time getting us to be honest ourselves. How can we bless others if we're still living in dishonesty ourselves? When people who need us come to us, are we ready to bless them? Are we ready to give to them? If we give to them what we are and what we have, is it worth giving?

We all need friends who are honest and straightforward. As the Bible states:

*Faithful are the wounds of a friend, but the kisses of an enemy are deceitful.*

Proverbs 27:6

If you're really my friend, you'll tell me the truth. If you're really my friend, you'll tell me to get my life together. Each of us needs a Nathan in our lives, someone who will not pull any punches, but will just let us have it.

After David had committed adultery with Bathsheba and had her husband killed to hide that fact, he was sitting on his throne one day like nothing had happened, when the prophet Nathan suddenly showed up. Nathan proceeded to tell David a story of a poor man who had possessed a single lamb, and that lamb had been taken from him by a rich man who already had many lambs of his own. When a visitor came, instead of using one of his own lambs, he had the only lamb of the other man slaughtered and cooked to feed the visitor.

When he heard it, this story so angered David that he said:

*As the Lord lives, the man who has done this shall surely die! And he shall restore fourfold for the lamb, because he did this thing and because he had no pity.*

2 Samuel 12:5-6

How shocked David must have been when Nathan responded:

*You are the man!*

2 Samuel 12:5-6

That's what we all need, someone who will get in our faces and tell us the plain truth. We all need to hear the truth—whether we like it or not.

If you love someone, you'll tell them the truth. If you're someone's friend, you'll tell them the truth. If you don't want someone to make a fool of themselves, you'll tell them the truth. And if you get your feelings hurt because someone close to you tells you the truth, then you're not worthy of their love. You don't deserve them as a friend or family member.

"You'd better get your act together!" Those are words that we all need to hear from time to time, and we cannot afford to despise the person who is honest enough to give them voice.

There are not nearly enough Nathans in this world, and many of us back away from those who do exist. We prefer to spend time with people who bow at our feet and tell us how wonderful we are.

The Nathans of this world would say to us, "You're not acting like a king; you're acting like a kid. You're much too selfish and lacking in self-discipline." And if we know what's good for us, we will thank the person who tells us that, and then we'll get busy bettering ourselves, instead of pouting and being offended at their "harsh" words.

You don't need people around you who let you settle for second best and congratulate you for every decision to be "normal." You need people around you who will constantly push you higher and not let you rest when you try to settle back and enjoy life.

If I'm wrong, I want someone to tell me I'm wrong. There's too much at stake, and my destiny is too important for me to be wasting time in insincerity.

We are not only unwilling to be honest with each other; we're even dishonest with God. This unwillingness to be honest with God is preventing some of us from experiencing a breakthrough in our personal lives. Tell the truth, and God will help you. Don't be afraid to confess all to Him. Pray prayers like these and watch Him work:

*"Lord, I have problems with my flesh. Please help me."*

*"Lord, I have a terrible temper. My father was the same way. Please release me from this generational curse."*

*"Lord, I'm struggling with an uncontrollable spirit of lust. I can't control my eyes, and my mind is in constant turmoil. Help me!"*

God will answer that kind of prayer because He blesses honesty wherever He finds it.

## JUSTICE

*Justice* is "the quality of being impartial or fair." What's right for one, is right for the other. You cannot, in this season, show partiality. There are no big I's and little you's. If it's right for me, then it's right for you too. And if it's wrong for me, then it's also wrong for you.

In the days of the Bible, right and wrong were clearly defined, and the blessing for right and the penalty for wrong were just as clear. God's Word declares:

*For the wages of sin is death, but the gift of God is eternal life in Christ Jesus our Lord.*

Romans 6:23

These words are just as true today as they were when they were written some two thousand years ago. The things that were wrong in Bible days are wrong now, and the things that were right in Bible days are still right. The fact that we're living in another era doesn't change anything. Justice is still justice. As it was then, so it is now.

*Justice* also means "righteousness, conformity to truth, fact, and reason." We need justice in this world, and we need justice on the inside of each of us.

The thing that is holding us back is not so much the disadvantage this world fosters upon us, as it is what's inside of us that no one else can see. We know it's there, and God knows it's there, but we have become experts at hiding it from the people around us. It's time that we admit our need and seek God's help.

It is time for truth and justice. What goes for one, goes for all.

For the most part, we treat people based on our opinion of them. But we can be wrong. So, as a Christian, allow God's impeccable sense of justice to prevail in your heart.


## KNOWLEDGE

Oh, please let this word *knowledge* become part of your everyday vocabulary. God doesn't want you to sound like everyone else around you because He's preparing you to relate to a whole different class of people. He's about to send you into new arenas, and there you will not be able to say just any old thing and be well received. You'll have to be able to think as the people around you think and talk as they talk.

You should get accustomed to wearing a business suit and carrying a briefcase, for I foresee you sitting at board tables and in conference rooms and serving as corporate executives. Some of you are destined to become millionaires. Some of you will stand before cameras and be interviewed, and on that day, you'll need to know how to talk properly.

God is trying to enlarge you so that He can raise you up, and you can't go into the Fortune 500 boardrooms with your Wal-Mart vocabulary. If you want to stay where you are, then be satisfied, but if you want to move on up, then stir yourself and make some changes. Gain the knowledge you need to prevail in other arenas.

*Knowledge* is "a result or a product of knowing information or understanding acquired through experience." God will sometimes let you cry so that you learn new things. In the process, He will let you go through situations and circumstances that will tempt you to doubt Him and His goodness. But His purpose in it all is for you to have greater knowledge.

You may well have been wondering why you're going through some of the things you're going through, but I can tell you the why of it. You're learning. That's why. Everything that you experience in life teaches you and makes you wiser and more able to help others.

*Everything that you experience in life teaches you and makes you wiser and more able to help others.*

What's bad is that sometimes we go through a terrible trial, and we learn nothing at all from it. The reason is that we gripe and complain so much about what we're experiencing that we don't have time to hear God's voice in the process. Always learn something from what you're experiencing, for experience is still the best teacher.

God is adding to you, enlarging you. He is so concerned about you that He allows you to go through things that seem severe. In the process, you might bend, but He knows that you won't break.

A mighty oak tree seems so much more substantial than a palm tree, but that theory is put to the test when hurricane-force winds come. In that moment, the limbs of the oak tree snap, but the palm tree, although it may bend to the ground, usually springs back.

Be like that palm tree, and bounce back. Learn something from the storms that assail you.

You may feel like the winds of adversity never let up on you. But they will eventually die down, and you'll be a better person for what you have suffered. Just bounce back, and bounce back stronger.

God is with you, so no winds of adversity can break you. Bounce back, and be wiser for your trial.

Yes, bounce back, and when you bounce back, be better then ever for God, stronger than ever. Be more courageous than ever and more tenacious than ever. Let your experience make you more effective for God. He said:

*So I will restore to you the years that the swarming locust has eaten, the crawling locust, the consuming locust, and the chewing locust, My great army which I sent among you. You shall eat in plenty and be satisfied, and praise the name of the Lord your God, Who has dealt wondrously with you; and My people shall never be put to shame.*

Joel 2:25-26

God has allowed whatever you've been gong through to happen, and He did it for a purpose. Now it's restoration time. Bounce back, and learn something from your experience.

Everything that you face in life has a purpose. God may be trying to teach you something about yourself. He may be trying to teach you something about other people. And He may be trying to teach you something about Himself. Imagine it! One simple trial can teach you so much! Learn to treasure every trial and to rejoice in it. God has a purpose for it and, through it, He's lifting you higher.

The devil is not nearly as intelligent as he thinks. If he wanted to destroy us, he would surely not want us to face trials and tests. They only strengthen us. And yet, he continues to submit us to one situation after another. What he intends for harm, God intends for our good. In the process, we're learning and we're growing. Satan wants to push us down, but the actual result is that we're rising higher.

Stop delaying and hindering the process, and let God increase you in knowledge and understanding as He desires to do.

## LOYALTY

This word *loyalty* is so foreign to us today that we rarely employ it in normal speech. It sounds almost archaic, like some long-forgotten concept. *Loyalty* means "fidelity, allegiance; the state, quality, or fact of being loyal," and we need a lot more of it these days.

Far too few modern Christians know anything about loyalty, but God requires it of those who hope to excel in this modern world. He requires loyalty to Him, to His precepts, and to His purpose. He also requires that we be loyal to one another. If you want to live "right" in this wrong world, you'll have to get this godly concept down into your spirit.

## MORALITY

The root of this word *morality* is *morals*, and the power of morals has declined seriously in our modern world. Morality speaks of "virtuous conduct," and this is what God is calling for in each of our lives.

*Morality* is also "a system of principles of right and wrong conduct; a code of ethics." Christians are called to change their lifestyle, to raise the level of their morality.

The morals that we strive for are based on the teachings of the Bible, but when convenience or comfort come into question, too often morals take a backseat. Many modern Christians, if they were told that they could rob a bank and get away with it, would be sorely tempted to try it. Their prime motive for not robbing a bank is not what it should be. We might imagine that their first thought would be not to dishonor God, but actually it is not to spend time in prison. When a thing is legal but immoral, many Christians succumb. In all of this, the real question is lost. And that question is: "What is right?"

A person of the world will do most anything they can get by with doing, but a Christian is called to take morality to the next level. We are called to do what is "right" in every situation. We are called to do "right" when others are present and watching, and also when no one is present and watching. If we want God's blessing, it's time to tighten up on loose living and show the world what true morality means.

## PHYSICAL APPEARANCE

Many Christians don't understand why physical appearance should be important to them. As Christians, are we not to be concerned for the spirit and the soul? Why, then, should we pay attention to our physical appearance? Why is it important to get this truth down into our spirits?

It's important because God wants to bring us to another level and to present us before a totally different group of people. He can't do that if we're not considered presentable to that group of people.

I'm not advocating vanity. This is not about getting stuck on yourself. It's about taking care of the temple God has chosen to dwell in.

Jesus taught:

*Let your light so shine before men, that they may see your good works and glorify your Father in heaven.*

Matthew 5:16

What's the first thing people notice when they look at you? It isn't your pure spirit. Believe me. Your physical appearance, for good or for bad, dictates first impressions. Therefore, we must be conscious of our physical appearance always.

As we have already seen, although you may not like the body God gave you and prefer to have another, it's the only body you'll ever have. So you'd better take care of it.

Plastic surgeons are fattening their bank accounts because many of us don't like our looks, and facelifts and other forms of cosmetic surgery have become rather commonplace. But if you don't take care of yourself, there's only so much a plastic surgeon can do to help you. When the body begins to break down, there's often not much you can do about it.

It's time to take physical fitness to a new level. For instance, it's time that each of us set aside sufficient time for rest. God established rest as a means of the body repairing and replenishing itself, and when you don't get enough rest, that repair process is frustrated.

But, surprisingly, one of the most important elements in physical fitness is spiritual fitness. The spirit affects the body.

It may sound foolish to some, but our daily devotions are actually part of our physical fitness. Because of this, we can't afford to shortchange God. If you need to get up fifteen minutes earlier in the morning to meet with Him, then do it. If you need to stay up thirty minutes after everyone else has gone to bed, then do it. This duty to God comes before job, house, spouse, children, or any other responsibility, and it will do more than anything else to affect your health and overall physical well-being.

Find a comfortable place where you can commune with God. It may be in the living room, the sitting room, or den, or it may even be in the bathroom. Do what is comfortable for you, but do it.

Most of us in our modern world are so over-committed that we rush from one thing to the next all day long and find, at the end of the day, that we're just too exhausted to give God the time He deserves. This is a serious mistake.

Oh, I know how it is. We're running late, and we can't find our shoes. Then we have to get the children together and out the door and to their place of activity. When we arrive at the office, coworkers seem to pop in and out all day long. We have special lunches, and by the time the work day is over and we're headed home, our heads are spinning so much that we're just hoping to get to bed as early as possible.

When, at last, our heads hit the pillow, we realize that another twenty-four hours have passed, and we have given time to everyone else but God. It is altogether fitting and proper that we spend time with family members and co-workers, but we cannot afford to neglect God.

I see people arriving hurriedly for our mid-week services, and I can't help but notice how haggard they appear. They sometimes nearly stumble into the building, exhausted from their hectic schedules.

Much of this is due to the fact that we have not disciplined ourselves to start every day off right, with a time of devotions in the presence of the Lord. In such a time of fellowship with Him, He can get you ready for all that you will face throughout the day. Instead, we feel exhausted, have bags under our eyes, and suffer from migraine headaches and high blood pressure because we haven't had enough time with God.

Too many of us are abusing and misusing this temple of ours. Even computers occasionally experience overload and shut down. What can you expect from your body over time? For your own good, bring some balance and some structure into your life.

Believe it or not, spending time in the presence of the Lord will keep you looking good. It will keep you more youthful. If you don't believe that, look at some of your co-workers or look at some of your old classmates who are still living in sin. Sin wears out the body and makes it look much older than it actually is. But the glory of God will preserve you and make you look years younger.

Give us more of Your glory, Lord.

When people look at us, they should see the glory of the Lord upon us, and the first indicator of this is our physical appearance. Keep it "right."


## PLEASURE

The average Christian has come to think of *pleasure* as a bad word, but it's not. We've been taught by well-meaning people that pleasure and sin are synonymous, but that's not necessarily so. God wants His children to experience pleasure in this life.

*Pleasure* can be defined as "an agreeable or delightful sensation, enjoyment, one's preference or choice." Walking in obedience to God and loving and serving Him does not mean that you cannot have pleasure in life. Jesus said:

> *I have come that they may have life, and that they may have it more abundantly.*
>
> John 10:10

God wants you to enjoy life. Too many Christians, once they get saved, go to the other extreme and forget how to have fun in life. We need some stress busters in our daily lives, some tension relievers. Most Christians feel that if they're beginning to have fun, something must be wrong, and they start repenting and asking God for forgiveness.

Have fun! Reward yourself once in a while. Have a slice of cheesecake with cherries on top, a big piece of key lime pie, or whatever it is that delights your palate. Believe me, there's nothing wrong with that.

Why is it that the average Christian is so uptight, so frustrated, and so overwrought? It's because they have no relief valve. When was the last time you took a day off just to pamper yourself? All of us need a little pampering occasionally. God wants us to live a righteous life, but there's nothing wrong with pampering yourself from time to time.

Do it. Say to yourself and anyone else involved, "This is *my* day, and I'm going to pamper *myself* all day long." You'll be surprised. It will do wonders for you.

When I attended one church, some time ago, the longer I sat there, the more depressed I felt. Everybody in that place seemed to be impatient and stressed out. They were just "suffering for Jesus" and hoping for the day when it would all be over. But this is not a time for sadness or despair. These are wonderful days that we should all be enjoying. Our enjoyment delights our heavenly Father.

Take some time and go to a park or lake area. Open your trunk, and let some music play like you did when you were still in the world. Take along several pounds of crayfish, some hot turkey necks, spicy sausage, corn on the cob, and some ice-cold Fruitopias, and you're ready to "chill." Take some of those Purple Passion drinks or Strawberry Integration, and have yourself a good time.

After working eight hours a day, fighting with countless demons and having to wrestle with your children, you need some relief. Do whatever it is that you enjoy the most. God wants you to do it, and He'll be pleased when you do.

Here's another idea: Pick up a couple of nice candles, and some bubble bath and lotion at your local Bath and Body Works and take them home with you. Then, after dinner, light those candles and settle down in the bathtub. Then use the body lotion and rejoice in the goodness of Jesus.

*Relax. It will do wonders for your attitude.*

Some of you husbands and wives just work and work, and that's all your lives are. Get yourselves some bicycles and go riding together. Here in New Orleans, a good place to ride is in the old French Quarter, the historic district of the city. Look for the bike paths in your city and then relax away all your tensions as you enjoy the scenery and the fresh air.

If you have young children, go to the store and buy a kite, and then take it out and fly it with them. They'll never forget it, and you'll feel younger too. Have a good time.

Many believe that after a person is saved it is wrong for them to have any type of pleasure, but they're sadly mistaken. We're God's children, and He wants us to "have a blast" as we go through this life.

Relax. It will do wonders for your attitude. It will greatly improve your witness. It will increase your patience. And, as we have noted, you'll even look better.

Some of us are aging much too fast. If you can learn to enjoy living, it will slow down that process considerably. After all, you can't be Superman all the time. You have to be Clark Kent every now and then.

Do you have a hobby? Do you have something you enjoy that helps you relax? I'm not talking about something that becomes an obsession and you spend every spare moment in life doing it. I'm talking about something that you do occasionally, perhaps on weekends.

Life, to many, seems like a punishment. "The daily grind" they call it. Even what we eat these days seems to be a punishment. There's nothing wrong with a low-carb diet, but once in a while, we should just forget the diet and have a good time. Eat what you like to eat. Eat what you enjoy, what tastes good to you. Reward yourself.

It's time to come out of the prison you have defined for yourself. If you let God free your mind, it could add years to your life and change it in many fruitful ways.

Once in a while, we each ought to buy a new pair of shoes and enjoy doing it. A woman should be able to go to the beauty salon and sit under the hair dryer and relax while someone else pampers her. Once in a while, she should enjoy a good scalp massage.

I'm sure that many of you are laughing as you read this, but it's no laughing matter that our lives have not been very enjoyable, very pleasurable. God wants this to change.

This word *pleasure* also means "one's preference, one's choice." There's nothing wrong with you driving your dream car if you can afford it. Don't try to hide your blessings because you're afraid of what people will say. If God's favor is on you, His favor is on you. So what? Go get what you want to get.

Your car doesn't have to be a Mercedes, but if that's your choice, and you're tithing and faithfully sowing your seed offerings, why shouldn't you have it? It's time for you to experience some pleasures in life, to have some of your preferences, your choices.

I have some leaders in my church who needed to hear this message. I had to inform them that they were spending too much time in the church. They didn't need to be in all nineteen services. They needed to get out to a Saints' football game once in a while or some other healthy diversion. We all need a balance of activities in our lives.

And I had to take a dose of my own medicine. I couldn't afford to allow the many activities of the ministry to kill me. I had too much to live for. It's time for God's children to take pleasure in His goodness and to begin to enjoy life.


## POWER

God has given us power, but most of us have not yet realized just how much power we have. The devil loves that. He wants to keep us ignorant on this point.

This word *power* means "the ability to act, capability, potential, the possession of control, authority, influence over others." Most of us back down way too fast when faced with life's difficulties. The truth is that we have the power on the inside of us to overcome whatever life throws our way.

You have in you the ability to act, the ability to make things happen. Yet, when some door seems closed to you, you become discouraged. Rather than becoming discouraged, look for another way. Look for an open window or another, greater door to open.

Until we can recognize the power within us, we cannot move into positions of leadership. God wants to place us before and over weaker individuals who can draw from our strength. Yet we feel that we can barely make it on our own. The truth is that you have enough power for yourself and to share with others.

God purposed you to be a man or woman of power and influence. When you look in the mirror every day, the person you see looking back at you may not seem to be a person of influence, but that's because you have not yet recognized the power of God that's resident in you. You have crammed your feet into a size 7 shoe and contented yourself with smallness, when God has destined you to be a size 10.

No wonder you're so uncomfortable! Your shoes are too small. Your world is too small. You're trying to be a follower, when God has called you to be a powerful leader. Since mere fellowship is more convenient than leadership, you have chosen the easy path. After all, leaders bear greater responsibility.

Stop complaining about the down payment you must make for leadership and start getting ready for the role God has destined you to play. He has placed the power in you. Now use it for His glory.

You have had some experiences that will be used to set others free. You have been through some things that the average person can't even imagine. And you can't just keep all of that to yourself.

The power is already on the inside of you because the Greater One has taken up residence in you (see 1 John 4:4). On the basis of God's promise in this regard, we might also say: "Greater is He that is in you than he that is after you." You have power.

Many of us have run from the devil when it came time for spiritual warfare. What a sight! The devil running after you, and you running from him!

Oh, he's after you all right. He's after you on your job, in your home, and wherever else you happen to be. He's working on your mind to make you believe that you cannot defeat him. But you can. God has given you the power.

So stop running, turn around, and face the devil. If you don't know who you are, he'll be glad to define you. But you can't afford to allow him to do that.

You should know and you should let him know that your mistakes of the past have nothing whatsoever to do with your promises for the future. Past mistakes never disqualify you. In fact, past mistakes, faults, and failures and how you overcome them qualify you for leadership positions. Because *you* have overcome, you're ready to help others overcome. God has given you that power. You've been through hell and high water, and now you're ready to lead others through their time of testing.

What you've been through makes you more serious for God. It makes you realize how great your destiny is. If Satan has fought you so hard, it must be because he knows your potential. When you come out on the other side, you have some dreams and goals to work toward, and you're not about to waste any more time. You're powerful, and Satan knows it.

This doesn't mean that the devil will now leave you alone. Not at all. He is not attacking you for what you currently are, but for what you can become in God. He knows that when you get to the top, you will reach down and pull up as many others as you possibly can. He knows that you will not just sit there arrogantly. You'll do all within your power to topple his kingdom.

Because of this, you make him very nervous. He's troubled about your great love for people, and he knows that you will help many if he ever lets you up. He knows how powerful you can be.

Something very interesting happened in the 2004 Summer Olympics. Our United States team won many gold medals, but our basketball team struggled from the beginning. In their very first game, against little Puerto Rico, they lost.

The amazing thing was that the Olympic team was made up of some of the greatest NBA stars in this country. There was Alan Iverson, Lebraun James, Stefan Mulberry, and a host of other superstars, all earning in the millions of dollars annually. Still, they were defeated several times by teams from rather poor countries.

The coach of the Olympic team, Larry Brown (a man who only weeks before had been named NBA Coach of the Year because his Detroit Pistons team had won the championship), was interviewed, and they asked him what the problem was with the U.S. team. His answer was interesting. He said, "As a coach, I can only do so much. I can coach execution, but I can never coach effort."

Wow! That spoke volumes. Those team members had explosive talent and a championship coach, but it was up to them to decide they wanted to win. The power was there. They just had to decide to use it.

God can't force you to go to the next level, but He is encouraging you to do it. If you're satisfied where you are, what can He do? If you're satisfied to wait for another time, what can God do? If you're satisfied to see others move ahead and you say behind, what can He do? He has made His power available to you. Now it's up to you what you do with it.

My feeling is that we've come too far to turn back now. Why not go all the way with God? Why not see what His endgame is?

We've made it over some pitfalls, and we have climbed and jumped over some of life's boulders. It's time to move on with power and with passion.

Passion has been all but lost in the Church. We have far too many choir members singing without passion and musicians playing without passion. We have preachers preaching without passion, ushers serving without passion, and far too many of our leaders are just going through the motions as well. It's time to grow up, to mature, and to put to work the explosive power that God has deposited into our lives.

# RECOGNITION

This is another word that must become part of our mindset and our vocabulary. We're familiar with the word *recognize,* and from it we get the word *recognition. Recognition* means "acknowledgment of a fact or claim; to be made to feel significant and important."

This works both ways. We need recognition, and in order to get the recognition we need, we must recognize and acknowledge others. There is a biblical principle that must be applied here:

> *Do not be deceived, God is not mocked; for whatever a man sows, that he will also reap.*
>
> Galatians 6:7

Many Christians are extremely gifted and talented. They are the right people for the job, and yet they're not doing much in the kingdom of God because no one has yet recognized them. This is a serious problem and one we need to find a solution to.

So how does one go about getting recognized? Galatians 6 shows us that the way you get recognition is by first recognizing others. God will bring before you some people who have been beaten down and destroyed, and He will call on you to recognize the goodness in them. He wants you to make those oppressed people feel significant. If you do this, in time, recognition will come to you too.

Are you making the people around you feel significant? Whatever you give out will come back to you.

You need to give others a chance. You need to give them the benefit of the doubt. Your coworkers may not seem to be as intelligent as you are, and they may not have been exposed to all that you have been exposed to, but you should be able to look on the inside of them and see something in them that they cannot see in themselves. When you do, begin to talk about it and work to bring it to the surface. They have a talent. Find it and utilize it.

Some of you who are gifted as managers are much too harsh in your treatment of others. All you ever do is correct; you never reward. Each of us needs a balance. Someone has made *you* feel significant. Someone has granted *you* recognition. And now you need to reciprocate by recognizing others.

We all need affirmation. We all need encouragement from someone who can see in us elements that are not being put to good use. We all need someone to look beyond our obvious faults, our flaws and failures, and see the greatness within us and then begin to call it forth.

A large part of what we do in our intimate relationships is to affirm each other. If that is not being done, the relationship is not a healthy one. Anyone who does not or cannot discern your worth as an individual is not worthy of you. Don't even think about entering into an intimate relationship with such a person. It's not your place to try to convince others of your significance. They should be convincing you.

Many people with whom you come in contact lack a sense of significance in their lives, and you have the opportunity to give it to them. You meet people with this need on the job, but you will also meet them in the course of your other daily activities. If you're so stressed out and concentrated on your own problems and needs that you can't see beyond them, you'll miss your opportunity. But if you can look beyond yourself (as you so desire others to do for you), you can change the lives of the people around you in dramatic ways. People need somebody to speak into their lives, and you can be that "somebody."

Many did not receive enough recognition as they were growing up. If, as an adult, they're still not receiving the recognition they need, that opens the door to every conceivable attack of the devil.

Sometimes we are only tolerated at home, but everywhere else we go we're celebrated. This is not a good feeling. All of us are more drawn to celebration than we are to toleration, and this can lead to some serious problems.

We preachers sometimes have a problem in this regard. Jesus said:

*A prophet is not without honor except in his own country and in his own house.*

Matthew 13:57

There was a time when I was flying here and there around the country, accepting any and every engagement, because I felt more appreciated in other cities and other churches than I did in my own church in New Orleans. When I went other places, and I spoke and said, "The Lord says that we should do this … ," the people accepted it as a word from God and acted on it immediately. I didn't feel that I was getting the same respect at home. In time, I recognized that the devil was using this to try to move me out of a blessed place.

Recognition is vitally important to every marriage. What's more, marriages in which the husband and wife no longer have fun together are in trouble. Our homes should be fun places. Grown-ups should get down on the floor sometimes and play with their children, acting crazy with them.

Our homes have become much too businesslike, a place to go and regroup for the next battle. What ever happened to fun? When was the last time you played Monopoly in your home? There's a kid inside of every king, and there's a king inside of every kid. Take time to play with the kings and queens God has placed under your care.

In every wholesome covenant relationship, there should be a balance. Have a ball in your house, and in the process affirm those whom God has placed in your sphere of influence.

## RESPONSIBILITY

Most of us understand this word *responsibility*, and yet for some reason, responsibility is sorely lacking in many Christians today. This is not right. A person is not living right when there's no sense of responsibility in their life.

*Responsibility* can be defined as "the state of being accountable," and many of us still don't want to be accountable to anyone. We don't want to take instruction, and we don't want to submit to others. When things are not done in the way we would do them, we rebel and, all too easily and quickly, walk away from our place of blessing—all because we don't want to be accountable.

*Responsibility* also means "answerable legally or morally for the discharge of a duty, trust, or debt." How can you be responsible if you're not willing for someone to delegate a duty to you? Somebody has to be in charge, and it can't always be you.

You have to be accountable to others—no matter how old you are, whether you're male or female, and whether you're black, white, or any other color. We all need someone to whom we are accountable, and this is something that we lack today in the body of Christ.

Far too many Christians join a church these days, but they stay there only as long as they're happy. The moment they get angry at something the preacher said or something someone in the choir did, they leave, without a word of explanation, and go elsewhere. There is in them no sense of responsibility or accountability. "No one will ever know," they reason within themselves, but God knows.

It's amazing how many treat their jobs in the same way. They arrive at work late, act abusively toward other employees, take too much time for lunch break, and do their work sloppily. Yet, the moment someone tries to correct them, they take it personally and either quit or make a terrible scene in the workplace.

Correction is not condemnation, and all of us need it from time to time. The Scriptures teach us:

> *For whom the Lord loves He chastens, and scourges every son whom He receives.*

> Hebrews 12:6

Stop feeling condemned every time you're corrected, and start praising God that He loves you enough to care about your welfare. He wants you to do things in the very best way, and so He must teach you what that best way is.

Solomon wrote:

*Do not correct a scoffer, lest he hate you; rebuke a wise man, and he will love you.*

Proverbs 9:8

I don't want someone telling me that I'm doing a good job when, in reality, I'm making a fool of myself. I want to hear it like it is. And many of us need to hear that we are sorely lacking when it comes to responsibility.

Become a responsible member of your church, and don't be a spiritual shoplifter, going to church to get what you want without being willing to carry your share of the burden. Some rush in, get fueled up, and then rush out again, and then they wonder why the principles they learned at church are not working for them in real life. They're not connected, and they have assumed no real responsibility. It's time for responsibility among mature and serious saints.

## SELF-DISCIPLINE

Before I even give the definition of this word, I can imagine some people saying, "Ouch." Right now, a wave of conviction may be washing over some who are reading this. You know you need more self-discipline. We all do.

*Self-discipline* is "to train to obedience, to train to subjection, a system or rules or method of practice." Every one of us needs to discipline our flesh, training it, forcing it, if necessary, to do something it doesn't want to do.

As an example, as we discussed a little earlier, we have to force ourselves to spend time with God in prayer—even when we don't feel like it. No sooner is it time to pray than we begin to feel very sleepy. Then, when we have gone to bed, we can't sleep.

This flesh of ours is "a mess," and it resists training and discipline. It wants to do what it feels like doing at the moment. A lack of self-discipline is one of the greatest things holding most of us back from achieving more in life. God wants to give us so much more and entrust so much more to our care, but He can't trust us yet.

When Jesus was on earth, He was living in the flesh of a man, and so He experienced the struggle with His flesh. As we have noted, His flesh didn't like what it saw when the Father held out the cup of suffering to be drunk. He had to force the issue:

*"O My Father, if it is possible, let this cup pass from Me; nevertheless, not as I will, but as You will."*

Matthew 26:39

He knew what needed to be done, but His flesh rebelled against it. So He forced His flesh to obey, bringing His soul and body under subjection to the Spirit. And that's exactly what we all have to do. For more on this all-important teaching, see Chapter 10.

Just tell your flesh, "Shut up! Hold your peace! Keep quiet!" And then you can go on and do what you know to be the will of God for your life.

Your flesh is a big baby, always wanting attention and always complaining about what it doesn't have, and you have to quiet it. Say to your flesh, "Oh, grow up!" I know that hurts, but it's necessary. The moment you are able to muster up more self-discipline, you will be greatly enlarged spiritually.

## WEALTH

Many Christians seem to say this word like they're afraid of it, but wealth is nothing to be afraid of. We should say the word like it's about to become a part of us, for that is our Father's will.

This word *wealth* means "affluence, an abundance of valuable material possessions or resources." That word *abundance* means "having more than you need, a surplus." In other words, God wants you to have enough for yourself and some left over for somebody else. Why should we fear that?

God's Word declares:

*And you shall remember the Lord your God, for it is He who gives you power to get wealth.*

Deuteronomy 8:18

Some of us are afraid of the word *wealth* because we think it just means rich, but you can be rich and still not be wealthy. There are other, more important, things in life.

Also there are levels of richness. For instance, Alex Rodriguez, who plays professional baseball for the New York Yankees, is rich. Derek Jeeter and Jason Giambi are also members of that team, and they're also rich. But George Steinbrener, the owner of the Yankees, is truly wealthy.

What's the difference? Although Steinbrener's players are rich, each of them is confined to a specific contract. Steinbrener, on the other hand, determines how much each player will receive. If he could pick up Alex Rodriguez from the Texas Rangers and pay him $125 million a year, how much must Steinbrener himself be worth? He is indeed wealthy.

Shaqueel O'Neal, one of the great stars of the National Basketball Association today, is very rich, but the owner of the Miami Heat who drew Shaq away from the Los Angeles Lakers is truly wealthy and could afford to pay Shaq what he was worth.

When speaking to us of wealth, God is not trying to draw our attention particularly to money. We're to be wealthy in so many other ways, as well—wealthy in peace, wealthy in love, etc. But money is important, and we all need it to live. Whatever you do, don't be afraid of the blessing God wants to send your way.


# WISDOM

This word *wisdom* should be self-explanatory. It means "knowledge, learning, practical judgment; insight; common sense." Wisdom and the need for wisdom is one of the most extensively developed biblical themes, and yet we Christians remain so very lacking in wisdom today.

Wisdom comes in several ways. (1) It can be learned through study. (2) It can be the result of living experiences. That's why older people are, in general, wiser than younger people. But it can also be received as a gift from God. He said:

*If any of you lacks wisdom, let him ask of God, who gives to all liberally and without reproach, and it will be given to him.*

James 1:5

Since God has all wisdom, Christians should be far and away ahead of anyone else in this regard. Our problem is, then, that we're not tapping into the resources available to us. If you want to live "right" in this wrong world, you will need to dedicate yourself to the acquisition of wisdom.

## WORK

Again, this word should be self-explanatory, but instead of something good, we often see work as something bad, something to be avoided. In dictionary terms, *work* simply means: "Continued exertion directed to some end, labor, toil, a feat or deed." Believe me, when I say that if you do not have a specific goal in mind, and if you are not making an effort to advance toward that goal, you will not achieve anything in life.

Work is a necessary element of accomplishment, and without a dedication to work, your life will have very little meaning. I urge you to get this concept planted deep in your spirit.

## THE CONCLUSION

So those are the twenty words I want you to get in your spirit: achievement, compassion, courage, creativity, faith, health, honesty, justice, knowledge, loyalty, morality, physical appearance, pleasure, power, recognition, responsibility, self-discipline, wealth, wisdom, and work. Place those twenty words within your spirit, keep them before your eyes, and meditate on them day and night, and they will ultimately become part of you.

God is stretching us and enlarging us, and part of that enlargement is the enlarging of our minds. We are seeing a dimension of Him that we've never seen before, and this is changing the way we think, speak, and act.

If you will allow it to, this teaching will totally transform your prayer life. Now, when you pray, you can know what to pray for, what to expect, and what to contend for. As these words become part of your prayer, your prayer life will be enlarged and enriched.

This new knowledge will expand your horizons in every sense of the word. Now, when you're talking to God, you won't have to wonder what to say.

Make a copy of these twenty words and put them on your refrigerator. Put them on your desk. Keep them before you and make them a part of you. These attributes must not only become part of our vocabulary; they must become a part of our psyche. We must meditate on these words, embrace them, begin to confess them, and make a home within our hearts for them. In this way, we will have made considerable progress toward *Doing "Right" in a Wrong World.*

# CHAPTER 8

# Doing the "Right" Thing
# by the Family

*Oh, that they had such a heart in them that they would fear Me and always keep all My commandments, that it might be well with them and with their children forever!*

Deuteronomy 5:29

Moses, the great leader of God's people during the Exodus from Egypt and the march toward the Promised Land, was giving his farewell address. He had not been able to bring the children of Israel into the land itself, and he didn't want his entire life's work to be in vain. He wanted to see the people inherit what had been promised to them, and he wanted them to prosper in their new land.

## THE IMPORTANCE OF THE FAMILY TO SOCIETY

In order for the nation of Israel to survive and prosper, Moses understood, they would need strong families. The family unit will always be the cement that holds any nation together, and when the family has lost its cohesiveness, it's just a matter of time before the entire society begins to disintegrate. Sadly, that's exactly what seems to be happening in America today. Anything that we can do to strengthen families will bless this nation and the world.

Moses was in tune with God, and he knew that if the enemy were to have success in pulling families apart, the entire nation would be threatened. Therefore families, Moses showed, must begin to give God honor and obedience. They must fear Him and keep His commandments, and when they did the "right" thing, He would guarantee their future, securing it *"forever."*

The devil has no power over a society whose members fear God and obey His commandments. The future of such people is sealed. But failing to honor God in this way opens the door to an uncertain future. Who knows what may happen to those who ignore God and fail to keep His commandments? Their future is very much in question.

Your prosperity in the future does not depend on the luck of the draw or on you encountering favorable circumstances along the way. You can prosper even in the toughest of times when your heart is set on God. Fear Him, reverence Him, and obey Him, and you are guaranteed success in this life—whatever comes your way.

This is an important message for America today, for the nation is in crisis. More than a hundred thousand of our children are behind bars in prisons across this land. Four out of ten children in America now live in broken homes. Sixty-five out of every thousand children between the ages of seven and eleven in this country have already received psychiatric treatment.

The average age of young people in this country beginning to smoke cigarettes has dropped from fourteen to ten. A million girls between the ages of twelve and seventeen in this great land of ours will get pregnant and give birth, and that's not even counting those who will have abortions. One out of every five American children has admitted to using drugs at least twice a week. And right here in the land of the free and the home of the brave there are ten million minors currently infected with venereal diseases.

Something has gone terribly wrong with the American dream, and I'm convinced that the thing that has brought it all on is the fact that parents have lost their fear of God and their resulting obedience to the commandments of His Word. The promise *"that it might be well with them and with their children forever"* is contingent upon men and women embracing God's call to fear Him and keep His commandments.

One of the most famous passages of the Bible (and one that is taken very literally and acted upon in a very practical way by the Jewish people) is found in Deuteronomy 6, in Moses' recounting of God's dealings with the children of Israel in the wilderness:

*Now this is the commandment, and these are the statutes and judgments which the Lord your God has commanded to teach you, that you may observe them in the land which you are crossing over to possess.*

Deuteronomy 6:1

There are some things we must do on our way to our promised land, and if we expect to possess our land and prosper in it, we will have to do them. The enemy will fight us tooth and nail, because he doesn't want to see us prospering, and he knows that we're closer now than we've ever been to living the lifestyle God has called us to. That's why he has thrown everything at us except the kitchen sink. He knows that if he doesn't stop us quickly, the things that we've been believing God for, for many years, will shortly be manifested.

## "GIVE ME TRANSITIONAL OBEDIENCE"

On our way to our promised land, we and our children must obey God's commandments, and if we choose not to do it, we won't be able to stay in the land. So God is saying, "Give Me wilderness obedience, and be blessed in the land. Give me transitional obedience, and be blessed when the victory comes."

You may not know it, but you're in a transition right now, and transitional obedience is one that is governed by the Word of God, even when it seems to conflict with what you actually see and feel.

Moses made this requirement even more clear:

*That you may fear the Lord your God, to keep all His statutes and His commandments which I command you, you and your son and your grandson all the days of your life, and that your days may be prolonged.*

Deuteronomy 6:2

When you make a decision to fear the Lord, to reverence Him, and to keep the commandments He has given to you, it's not just for your sake. What you do will affect your children and grandchildren. As your children and grand-children learn to honor and obey God, their lives will be prolonged as well.

There's more:

*Therefore hear, O Israel, and be careful to observe it, that it may be well with you, and that you may multiply greatly as the Lord God of your fathers has promised you—"a land flowing with milk and honey."*

Deuteronomy 6:3

*"That you may multiply greatly."* God has promised us increase. We're not to stay where we are. We will continue to have everything we need, but there will be more, more than enough.

I love this word *multiply*, and I love it even more when it's connected with the word *greatly*. God has promised that we will *"multiply greatly,"* and He has prom-ised us *"a land flowing with milk and honey."* That's about as good as it gets.

So how do we secure our families in such a land with such an increase? There is something that we must *"hear"*:

*Hear, O Israel: The Lord our God, the Lord is one!*

Deuteronomy 6:4

God has something to say to us that will prepare us to move into the Promised Land and to prosper there. There is something that is required of us. What is it? It is to be found in the very next verse:

*You shall love the Lord your God with all your heart, with all your soul, and with all your strength.*

Deuteronomy 6:5

This should not surprise us. It's the very same message again. Our love for God should be very evident to everyone around us. It should be in our hearts, in our minds and wills (our souls), and even be manifested in our physical bod-ies, in our strength. Loving God causes you to exude some special energy. But here in America, I'm afraid, most of us no longer love God with all of our hearts, all of our souls, and all of our strength. We have lapsed into serving and worshipping Him when it's convenient for us to do.

When we love Him, His Word is in our hearts:

*And these words, which I command you today, these words must be in your heart.*

Deuteronomy 6:6

It's not enough that we attend church services just because a title requires us to perform a certain function there. We must attend because we love the Lord with all of our hearts, with all of our souls, and with all of our strength, and because His Word is in our hearts.

We are to love God even when we don't understand Him, even when we occasionally feel as though we have been abandoned by Him. We are to love Him because we know that He is faithful and trustworthy—whether we understand what He's currently doing in our lives or not.

Later, when we look back, we'll see the marks of an invisible hand protecting us, providing for us, and opening doors before us. Others will wonder how and why this happened, but they do not know about the time we have spent in the secret place with God.

As God promised, when we spend time with Him in secret, He rewards us openly:

*But you, when you pray, go into your room, and when you have shut your door, pray to your Father who is in the secret place; and your Father who sees in secret will reward you openly.*

Matthew 6:6

## SOME OF YOU ARE STANDING FIRM

Some of you who are reading this book have the devil very upset and confused. He's about to back off from you because he has come to realize that he'll never get you to turn your back on God. You won't turn back because you know there's nothing to turn back to. You've seen the light at the end of the tunnel, and you know that your victory is coming.

Some of you are in a position you've never been in before because your love for God has matured. The thoughts you're having are thoughts you've never had before, and you suddenly find yourself saying and doing things you've never said and done before. You now realize how childish and foolish it was to allow your-

103

self to be easily pulled off of the Potter's wheel before He was finished with you, and you're determined to let Him have His way with you now.

You now have some staying power because that was then, and this is now, and you suddenly realize that you're too close to turn back. And that's good news. This kind of love for God will affect all those around you. It will change your children and your grandchildren. My children know well that I'm human, but they also know that I'm no phony. They know that God is real in my life, and that fact can't help but affect them for the future.

*If we love the Lord and we want the best for our children, we'll teach them on a daily basis.*

## WHAT ARE WE PASSING ON TO OUR CHILDREN?

When was the last time your children had to apologize because they walked in on you while you were praying or reading the Bible? When was the last time you made an effort to instill the Word of God into them? If we love the Lord and we want the best for our children, we'll teach them on a daily basis.

If parents don't love God with all of their hearts, souls, and strength, then nothing good will be passed on to future generations. In this case, the enemy has won.

Not only are we to keep God's words in our hearts. There's more:

*You shall teach them diligently to your children, and shall talk of them when you sit in your house, when you walk by the way, when you lie down, and when you rise up.*

Deuteronomy 6:7

What are we to teach? The commandments and the statutes of God.

Every time you come home, the Word of God should be in your mouth. It should be there when you sit down with your family for dinner, when you're getting ready for bed, and when you kiss your family goodnight. Then, when you wake up every morning, God's Word should be in your mouth.

This is the life God is calling you to. It's time to rise a little higher, to seek God a little more diligently, to become a little more God conscious. It's time to love the Lord with your heart, your soul, and your strength, to have His words in your heart and to share them with those around you.

## SUCCESS IS GUARANTEED IF WE'RE WILLING TO CHANGE

God has provided a formula for the future success of your family, and although we thank Him for what we have accomplished until now, it's nothing compared to what He has for us just ahead. If you notice that your life seems to be filled with change, that's good. We all need change.

In fact, God wants to bring about so much change in our lives that as we are adjusting to a new change, that change will begin to change. You have to learn to move with the changes God brings and not get stuck in the past. God is changing, and if you don't get with the change, you'll be left behind.

We're all changing—whether we like it or not. If you're alive, you can't stay the same. For instance, your body doesn't look the same as it did ten years ago. It's constantly changing, and if it stops changing, that will probably mean that you're already dead. Change is necessary and good. Don't resist it. Flow with it.

The world around us is also changing. Some remember when there was no television, no contact lenses, no credit cards, no ballpoint pens, or no laser disks. Some remember a time when there was no penicillin, no frozen dinners, no radar, no panty hose, and no polio shots. Some of us were born before there was such a thing as birth control pills, before there were machines known as dishwashers. We were the dishwashers back then.

Many remember the advent of microwave ovens, the time when gays had no rights, when day care centers didn't yet exist and when FM radio was just a dream.

Back in the 1940s when something was labeled, "Made in Japan," it was considered junk. Now that's no longer true.

When I was growing up, *crack* meant a hole in the wall, *pot* was something you cooked in, *grass* was something you had to cut every weekend, and *AIDS* referred to helpers in the principal's office. Now all of those words mean something else entirely. Things are constantly changing.

Our generation believed that you had to have a husband to have a baby, but that's no longer the case. Many single women today have children and raise them on their own.

The many changes that have swept over our world in recent years have wreaked havoc on many lives, leaving behind those void of technical savvy. What has helped some of us to survive, even without great educational skills, is that our mamas taught us to fear God. "Always put God first," they taught us. "Never play around with Him."

When Sunday morning arrived, no one asked if we were going to church. If we wanted to live in our parent's house, eat their bread, and drink their water, we had no choice. Nowadays, parents complain that they can't do anything with their children. Why not? If they're living under your roof, sleeping in your bed, eating your food, and drinking your water, they're still under your control, and you'd better let them know that they will serve the Lord—or else.

## JOSHUA SPOKE FOR HIS WHOLE FAMILY

Joshua spoke for his whole family:

*As for me and my house, we will serve the Lord.*

Joshua 24:15

What's wrong with taking that same stand in the twenty-first century? If you fail to take such a stand, how do you expect your children to survive? What assurance do you have that they will survive? If they're allowed to walk through spiritual minefields, life may blow up in their faces at any moment.

If you fail to convey God's message to your children, they'll have no hope. A subtle anti-God message is being relayed to them daily through the popular media, and if you allow them to spend untold hours in front of the television, what can you expect the outcome to be?

The national beer industry will never tell you this, but they're investing billions of dollars every year in advertising so that when your child gets old enough to drink, doing so will seem to them to be a logical and desirable step. It is said that ninety-five percent of all college students in America now drink beer and, not surprisingly, beer consumption in America has risen to the unheard-of level of thirty-two gallons per capita per year. Since I don't drink any, that means that someone out there drinks sixty-four gallons a year or more. No wonder people act so crazy!

One study determined that eighty-eight percent of all sexual encounters portrayed on television are outside of matrimony. Modern movies very rarely show sexual intimacy between husbands and wives. Men seem to always be looking to their secretary or someone around the corner to meet their sexual needs—and now it's the same for women.

Can you see what's happening? The popular media is creating a certain mindset in our children, and therefore it's normal for your children to say, when they have reached adulthood, "I need a drink." May God help us. Will this generation survive? Not if we have not taught them God's ways. We must teach our children, just as our parents taught us.

God has promised our families a future, but the requirement is clear. It's up to us now to give Him the honor due to His name and to teach succeeding generations to do the same. Our teachings will lay the foundations for good things to come.

## LAYING FOUNDATIONS FOR GOOD THINGS TO COME

The beauty that initially attracts a man and a woman to each other is only skin deep, and unless there's something more sure upon which the couple can develop their life together, they could eventually become just two miserable people living in the same house. Don't risk building your house on sand. Begin laying a proper foundation for it today.

Do whatever you have to do. Drive in some pilings, lay a concrete slab, or pour footers and lay some blocks. Have a formal groundbreaking, but then expect some hard work to take place before you can see something substantial rising from the site.

Many of us get very excited when it's time for a building project to begin. We're ready to see some lovely windows and doors put into place. But a lot of work is needed before we can advance that far. First, prepare a proper foundation, and then anything can be built upon it.

The only proper foundation for a family is sincere love for God. Without that, you won't have much to work with. And you won't have much of a chance to be blessed either. The goal of having a happy family will become, for you, just a mirage, an unobtainable dream.

Without the love of God as its foundation, no marriage can succeed, and no family can prosper. And without the love of God as its foundation, no society can work together toward a brighter future.

One of our problems in the modern world is that many feel they can't find time for God. Can't find time for God? You'd better *make* time for Him. This may sound, to some, like an old-fashioned concept, but believe me, nothing could be more important. If we hope to have a future, we have to go back and make sure our foundation is solid.

*Serving God should always cost you something...*

Just as Moses taught that we must love God with all of our hearts, all of our souls, and all of our strength, Paul said that he *"press[ed] toward the goal"*:

*I press toward the goal for the prize of the upward call of God in Christ Jesus.*

Philippians 3:14

Loving God and serving Him pulls you and your whole family up emotionally, and it pulls you all up physically and financially as well. At the same time, loving God and serving Him requires a certain exertion of emotional, physical, and financial energy on the part of each member of the family.

Serving God should always cost you something, and those who serve Him only when it's convenient for them to do so miss His very best. The man who has a new car and is even now on his honeymoon can always testify to the goodness of God, but what about four years from now when his Little House on the Prairie has turned into Nightmare on Elm Street? If you feel that God is still worthy to be praised, even though folks have been smiling in your face and stabbing you in the back at the same time, then you've grown spiritually. Pass this maturity on to the whole family.

If people have hurt you (and it happens to all of us to one degree or another), expect something good to come of it. It may be that God is about to place you in a position of leadership, and you can say, "I will never treat people the way others have treated me." Then reach down and lift others up with you as you rise. This includes the other members of your family.

## WHEN YOUR CHILDREN ENCOURAGE YOU

This works both ways. You're a blessing to your children, but they're also a blessing to you. When you're weary and need encouragement, the Lord will send it to you from the most unexpected sources. Sometimes that will include your own children.

Recently, my eight-year-old son Trey, who is now a red-belt karate senior, said to me, "Dad, you've just got to be at my tournament."

"I'll be there," I said, and I made sure nothing else interfered with that promise. But when the day arrived, I just happened to be feeling about as low as I had felt all year long.

When Trey and I arrived at the place of the tournament, he got out and went around to the back of the car and motioned to me with his hands in a folded pattern. I thought it must be one of his karate moves he was practicing in preparation for the event, so I just looked at him.

"Daddy," he said, a little exasperated, "Let's pray."

And with that simple gesture by my son, my spirits were lifted. If my eight-year-old son knew that without prayer to God he could not expect victory in a sporting event, what did I have to worry about?

Just be sure you do your part. You hold the key. You have what your family needs. You know what they need to know. You've seen what they need to see. You've heard what they need to hear. And you're going where they can't yet go, but you must insist on taking them along with you.

God has a very precise prescription for the family, and it's found right here in verse 6: *"And these words which I command you today shall be in your heart"* (Deuteronomy 6:6). *"These words,"* the words that God has commanded, must be in our hearts, not just in our mouths. If they're in our hearts, then they will come out of our mouths (and our children and grandchildren will be affected by them), but if they're only in our mouths and not in our hearts, then they're mere words.

## BECOME AN INTERCESSOR FOR YOUR FAMILY

I urge you to learn to intercede for your family. Pray, not only for your own children and grandchildren, but for other members of your family. For instance, pray for your aunts and uncles. Pray for your nieces and nephews. Some of them don't have godly parents, and they need your intercession. You may have to spiritually adopt some other family members and let them "hang out" with you so that they can learn God's ways and be blessed.

Pray for your brothers and sisters. The devil is intent on robbing them of the fear and reverence of God, and you must stop him. If you still have parents and grandparents, by all means, pray for them.

But don't think that prayer is enough. Set a godly standard for your family, abide by it yourself, and expect them to abide by it.

As we were growing up, we were not allowed to sit on the church steps or play at the front of the sanctuary. We had to respect God, and we had to respect His house. We were not permitted to chew gum in church. And we would never have dared to eat a morsel of food without first giving thanks to God and blessing it.

At the family dinner table, each of us gave a prayer of thanks for the food, and each of us quoted a Scripture verse. If we didn't want to do it, then we didn't eat. Today some parents don't know the promise of John 3:16, and some grandparents can't quote the 23rd Psalm. This is not right. God's Word declares:

*A good man leaves an inheritance to his children's children.*

Proverbs 13:22

This is not about being perfect; it's about representing God and being His spokesperson to those who don't know Him. If God has given you a child, then He has made you His heavenly representative to that child. That child will be introduced to heaven's ways through you—that is through your words and through your lifestyle.

As Moses said, *"And these words which I have commanded you today shall be in your heart; you shall teach them diligently"* (Deuteronomy 6:6-7). This word *diligently* means consistently. *"These words,"* God's words, must consistently be in your heart. The reason is that children can easily spot a phony. They must see that you not only speak the words, but also that you live the life. You not only go to church on Sunday; you live for God the rest of the week.

Your home must be known as a Christian home. That must begin with the contents of the home—what it has and what it doesn't have. Every Christian home must have a Bible placed so that it's clearly visible and accessible. It might be kept in the kitchen where everyone spends a lot of time, or in some other room where there are comfortable chairs where someone can sit and read it.

Many Christian homes have a copy of the Ten Commandments displayed prominently. Don't get so design conscious that you shut God out.

At Beacon Light Cathedral, we're pressing our people for lifestyle changes that will cause them to shine brighter, not only to their own families, but also to the world around them. Here in New Orleans, throughout America and the world, far too many Christians are Christian in name only, and that has to change.

They're saved, but they spend more time with their R&B collection than they do worshiping God. Christian homes need to have Gospel CDs with worship music playing. Such music brings the presence of the Lord into our homes. Far too few Christians are investing in good books, cassette tapes, and videos. After the nails and hair are done and some new clothes are bought, there's nothing left over for things that will edify us. Invest in your spiritual growth and development.

What station is your car radio set on? What do you listen to as you're on your way to church? It's time to love God with all your heart, all your soul, and all your strength. It's time to pay whatever price is necessary to serve Him so that the future of your family can be secure.

In this way, you *"learn to do well,"* and are able to go about *Doing "Right" in a Wrong World.*

# CHAPTER 9

# Doing the "Right" Thing by the Lost

*But even if our Gospel is veiled, it is veiled to those who are perishing, whose minds the god of this age has blinded, who do not believe, lest the light of the gospel of the glory of Christ, who is the image of God, should shine on them.*

2 Corinthians 4:3-4

God's Good News has been revealed to you through the teaching and preaching of His Word, and it's that Good News that has brought you to another level of living. But if this Good News, that now has become *your* Good News, is not shared with those who don't yet know what you know, then your Gospel is hidden, and men and women will perish as a result.

Every one of us has been destined to bless others. God saved you (and He most assuredly used some other person or persons to do that) so that you could help others to be saved. You're blessed so that you can be a blessing. As we have seen, God promised Abraham:

*I will make you a great nation; I will bless you and make your name great; and you shall be a blessing. I will bless those who bless you, and I will curse him who curses you; and in you all the families of the earth shall be blessed.*

Genesis 12:2-3

Jesus Himself said this:

*Let your light so shine before men, that they may see your good works and glorify your Father in heaven.*

Matthew 5:16

Too often, even after we have been saved, we're so consumed with our own needs that we miss opportunities to help meet the needs of those around us. But that's not "right" living. Someone who is concerned with "right" living takes on the responsibility of telling others the Good News that set them on the right path.

How can those who are perishing know about Christ's salvation if you don't tell them? Such people are found in your place of work, in the places you frequent for business and pleasure, in the restaurants where you enjoy eating, in the homes of your immediate neighborhood, and even in your own home.

A perishing person may even be lying in bed beside you or sleeping in the next room. If Jesus came today, that person would have to spend eternity in hell. So what are you waiting for? Tell them the Good News that saved you, and help them to be saved too.

Every man, woman, boy, and girl must face eternity. Some will spend it in the bliss of God's presence, and others will spend it in the torment of Satan's cauldron. You could make the difference for many.

"But," you might say, "they're sinners, so they deserve to go to hell." Well, you were a sinner too, but God saved you. And it doesn't matter how serious their sin might be. The greatest sin of all is not to believe on Jesus and accept Him as Savior. And if God could save you, He can save others.

## EVANGELISM HAS BEEN RELEGATED TO THE FEW

Evangelism in the twenty-first century has been relegated to the church building, and that's unfortunate. "If we can build an attractive enough building in a good location and lure sinners to it," we reason, "they will surely be changed." This is not biblical thinking.

Studies have shown that location has very little to do with whether or not men and women attend church services. And, anyway, there's nothing in the Bible that directs sinners to go to church. Nothing!

Rather than wait for sinners to come to the church, we're directed by the Lord to go out where they are and win them to Christ. They're not to come to us; we're to go to them. Yet the sad truth is that only about five percent of all Christian believers can say that someone, even one person, is following Jesus today because of their efforts.

*We call these buildings churches, but in reality it's the people who make up the Church.*

Evangelism, instead of the all-consuming passion of every believer, as it was intended to be, has become a ministry within the church, a ministry of a handful of people at best. God intended for every born-again believer to be an evangelist. If we have come out of darkness into the marvelous light of God, then it's our duty to tell others about that glorious light.

The mission given to us by the Lord is not just to put up church buildings. It's to form, from the unsaved and unchurched around and among us, congregations of new believers to inhabit the church buildings. And the people, the congregations, are always much more important than the buildings. We call these buildings churches, but in reality it's the people who make up the Church. The buildings will one day turn to ashes, but the people will live on throughout eternity.

The vision God has given us as a church organization is not just to place our organizational name on buildings in different cities. It's to win the lost in those cities, thus affecting cities, states, the nation, and the world for the Lord Jesus Christ. We want to change the eternal destiny of as many men and women as possible. This is our assignment. This is what we've all been called to do.

Your faith was meant to be contagious, and if it's not, it's probably contaminated. There should be something about your lifestyle that speaks to the people with whom you interact on a daily basis. When people have any interaction with you at all, it should make them want what you have. They should see in you excellence, maturity, love, righteousness—and much more, and these things should then rub off on them.

Our parents and grandparents were often heard to quote sayings like, "Birds of a feather flock together" and "Show me your company, and I'll tell you who you are." They meant that the fact that God had saved us should affect everyone we come in contact with.

## "COMPEL THEM TO COME IN"

When people hear the Gospel, they respond in various ways. In His parable of the great supper, Jesus taught:

*A certain man gave a great supper and invited many, and sent his servant at supper time to say to those who were invited, "Come, for all things are now ready." But they all with one accord began to make excuses.*

*The first said to him, "I have bought a piece of ground, and I must go and see it. I ask you to have me excused."*

*And another said, "I have bought five yoke of oxen, and I am going to test them. I ask you to have me excused."*

*Still another said, "I have married a wife, and therefore I cannot come."*

*So that servant came and reported these things to his master.*

*Then the master of the house, being angry, said to his servant, "Go out quickly into the streets and lanes of the city, and bring in here the poor and the maimed and the lame and the blind."*

*And the servant said, "Master, it is done as you commanded, and still there is room."*

*Then the master said to the servant, "Go out into the highways and hedges, and compel them to come in, that my house may be filled."*

Luke 14:16-23

This *"master"* represents Jesus, and here He was assigning men and women to recruit individuals to come to a great supper He had prepared. Everything was ready. The only thing lacking were the guests.

The first man who was invited made an excuse as to why he could not come, and the second did the same. When the third man began to make excuses, the master became angry.

116

Why was He angry? He knew that what the people outside needed was contained within the house, and it saddened Him that they would make excuses and not take advantage of His provision.

Then He directed them: "Just go out and get anyone you can find, anyone you can see along the way. Let them know that all things are ready, and they're welcome—regardless of their bloodlines, regardless of their past, regardless of the mistakes of their yesterdays."

So forceful was Jesus in all of this that He said at last: *"Compel them to come in that that my house may be filled."* What great desire on the part of our Lord! As His children, this is our assigned task in life.

## WHOSE JOB IS IT TO WIN SOULS?

It's not the pastor's job to win souls. He, as a believer in Christ who loves lost people, should do it. But every other believer should do it too. And when a pastor wins souls, it shouldn't always be through the pulpit. He should be winning souls wherever he encounters them, and you should too.

A pastor's job is to shepherd the flock, not to give birth to the lambs. The shepherd leads the sheep, but it's the responsibility of the sheep to produce more sheep. The pastor is to teach and instruct his members, so that they're edified and matured through the Word to the point that they can reach out to others around them. But he's not the evangelist, or, at least, the only evangelist. His job is to prepare all the members to be the evangelists as well.

Every deacon, every usher, every choir member, and every other member—whether performing some function in the church or just seated in the pew—has the responsibility of winning souls for the Lord by sharing the Good News of what Christ has done in their life.

## DON'T BLAME SINNERS FOR SINNING; JUST SHOW THEM A BETTER WAY

You can't just blame people who are walking in sin. Did you tell them any different? Did you show them a better way?

Don't blame them for being in sin. That's what sinners do. If you didn't have the Lord by your side, you wouldn't be doing well either. If you didn't have Him to call on in your moments of crisis, you wouldn't know where to turn either. Don't leave people in the dark where you once resided. Tell them about the light that has come into your life.

All of us know that if it were not for the Lord we could not have endured what we've gone through, so what do we expect of others? We know that our secret Source has been our salvation over and over again, and it's wrong not to share that insight with others. They need it just as we needed it.

If it had not been for the Lord, you would have given up long ago. Tell this to others who have not had the strength you found in Christ. If you had not felt the Lord walking close by your side, you might have lost your mind long ago. Tell others who are on the brink of insanity that there is Good News, and tell them before it's too late.

How can others be expected to handle adversity the way we Christians do? Even with Christ living on the inside of us, we know that sometimes life has been rough for us. Living for the Lord and with the Lord is sometimes challenging. What would it be like living without Him and without real purpose in life?

Don't be turned off by what sinners do. All of us live in the flesh, and the flesh can sometimes be selfish and demanding. Tell others what helped you overcome the flesh and its demands on you, and help them to be free of its demands on them too.

Don't be surprised when sinners are selfish. That's their nature. No one has to teach a small child selfishness. They just learn it on their own, or better said, they're just selfish by nature. No one has to teach them how to swear and be mean. It just comes to them naturally. They need Christ to change them, just as you needed Christ to change you.

Who taught children to scream when they want attention? They know when they're hungry, when they need to be changed, or when they just need to be comforted. And they instinctively realize how to make those feelings known. That's their nature. Don't be turned off by it.

The Bible lets us know that we are all born *"in sin"* and *"shapen in iniquity,"* (Psalm 51:5, KJV), but Jesus came so that we could be saved. Everything that He has done for us has to be shared with others. If we fail to do that, then we're the selfish ones.

## IT'S TIME TO SHARE OUR FAITH

Christian's who refuses to give of themselves will never go to the level God has destined them for. Serving God costs something, and, as much as we hate it, it involves that dreaded word *sacrifice*. The master commanded his servants: *"Go out into the highways and hedges and compel them to come in, that My house may be filled."* So what are you waiting for?

The Lord spoke to me at the end of 2003 to have a special gathering every fifth Sunday night in our New Orleans church and to invite the people from our various outreach churches and ministries to join us. This was not only to be a time of fellowship. We were to believe for a hundred souls from our particular city to be saved that day. We called this program Impact 100. A hundred souls saved would surely make an impact on any community.

Our thrust at Beacon Light Cathedral has been not just to get people to join us, but to get them saved, to change their eternal destination. That's our purpose in life. That's what God has saved us and called us for.

Some people in our modern world consider it to be an insult to tell others how they should be living, to suggest to them that we have a better way, and this has silenced many good Christians. But it is always "right" to tell people the truth. Whether they accept it or not is up to them, but if you tell them, at least you have fulfilled your obligation.

It's "right" to tell people about the *"wages of sin" and "the gift of God"* (Romans 6:23). It's "right" to tell people about Satan's true intentions in their lives and to contrast that with Christ's offer of *"life more abundantly"* (John 10:10).

It's "right" to let people know that the devil is not playing games. His work is deadly serious, and they need to know that the choices they make now will impact them for all eternity. They need to know that Satan wants to steal their vision, kill their hope, and destroy their dreams. Let men and women know that you're standing only by the grace of God, and that His grace is also sufficient for them.

There are not enough Christians who understand the seriousness of this hour, so how can we expect sinners to understand? Tell them. Make them understand. Compel them to come in.

## HE WHO WINS SOULS IS WISE

*The fruit of the righteous is a tree of life, and he who wins souls is wise.*

Proverbs 11:30

What we do will impact future generations. When we choose to live "right," our offspring will be blessed. This is why we must choose to do the "right" thing in every situation. And the beautiful part is that we have the opportunity to win souls through all of this.

God said, *"He who wins souls is wise,"* and that's a powerful statement! A wise man or woman is concerned about more then themselves; they're concerned about those around them. This includes the lost.

The fruit of the godly life is that others will come to Christ because of us— because of what we do and because of what we say. And this demonstrates wisdom.

What is wisdom? We looked at the full definition of this word in Chapter 7, but to me, wisdom is just good sense. When I'm in a given situation, good sense tells me what to do to achieve the best outcome. It lets me know what the consequences of my decision will be and forewarns me not to take certain paths. That way, I quickly know what I should do.

Each of us needs more wisdom, and it's not hard to get. You don't have to go on a long fast or speak in tongues for hours to get wisdom. It's in God, and He's in you, so weigh all the pros and cons of a situation, and then make your decision based on the good sense God gives you.

Still, the writer of the Proverbs added to that understanding of wisdom, when he stated, *"He who wins souls is wise."* The fruit of the godly life is leading others to Christ, and wisdom is the characteristic of a soul winner.

Some people have many academic degrees and also seem to have great spiritual insight. They can speak intelligently of the visions of Daniel and the revelation of John that seem so mind-boggling to many of us. People like that can literally astound others with their biblical knowledge. Still, in God's eyes at least, they're wise only if they're winning the lost around them.

Every one of us will one day have to stand before God and be judged. Some of us are convinced that this is the reason we must do many "good" things here on earth. But the truth is that in that day we will be rewarded, not on the basis of our goodness, but on the basis of how much we have allowed God to use us here on earth. What we have done will have little value then, but what He has done through us will count for all eternity.

Surprisingly, many who will seem to have valid reasons to be approved on that day will not be approved. Jesus said it Himself:

*Not everyone who says to Me, "Lord, Lord," shall enter the kingdom of heaven, but he who does the will of My Father in heaven. Many will say to Me in that day, "Lord, Lord, have we not prophesied in Your name, cast out demons in Your name, and done many wonders in Your name?" And then I will declare to them, "I never knew you; depart from Me, you who practice lawlessness!"*

Matthew 7:21-23

*"I NEVER KNEW YOU!"* What terrible words to have to hear from God! Going to church every Sunday is not everything. Singing in the choir is not everything. Volunteering time to the church is not everything. Even giving in the offering at church is not everything. Only those who win souls are counted as wise.

When you get to heaven, will others be there because you told them the Good News? Will men and women escape the flames of hell because you told them the Good News? That's what's important.

On that great judgment day, the average Christian will surely hang their head in shame. Looking over their shoulder, they will see no one following them. They may have attended conferences and bought teaching tapes, and yet they have never spoken to any lost soul about Christ.

## SHARE IT WITH OTHERS

Most of us have gone to some new restaurant, and the food was so good that we couldn't help telling others about it. Most of us have gone to some vacation spot, and we enjoyed it so much that we couldn't help telling others about it. And yet, when it comes to the most important thing in life—the difference between eternal salvation and eternal damnation—we're strangely silent.

The psalmist declared:

*Oh, taste and see that the Lord is good; blessed is the man who trusts in Him!*

Psalm 34:8

If we've recommended restaurants, hotels, parks, and scenic places to our friends, how can we not recommend Jesus to them? How can you not tell your coworkers His Good News? How can you not tell your friends what God has done for you? How can you remain silent?

## WHY YOU?

Satan has lied to us and told us that because we're less than perfect ourselves we should keep silent about the Savior, that we're not a worthy witness for Him. But that has nothing to do with it. The fact that the Lord has looked beyond our faults and seen our needs shows that He'll do the same for others. If God wanted perfect creatures to be His witnesses, He would have assigned the angels to do this work of evangelism.

*Being in Christ doesn't mean that you're perfect. It means that you're forgiven....*

We may not be perfect yet, and we may sometimes stumble and fall, but we know what to do when it happens. We know who to call on. We know where to turn.

God's Word declares:

*If we confess our sins, He is faithful and just to forgive us our sins and to cleanse us from all unrighteousness.*

1 John 1:9

Being in Christ doesn't mean that you're perfect. It means that you're forgiven, and you have a Friend by your side who helps you every moment of every day. It means that, in spite of your failures, you will spend eternity in heaven—because of His goodness, not your own. So you have every right to tell this Good News. Go out and compel others to come in.

Who are these "others"? They're your coworkers, your neighbors, your relatives, your friends, any and everyone with whom you come in contact.

Admittedly, some of us are not very good at one-on-one evangelism, and we need the help of those who are more gifted in this area. If that's true in your case, then take your friend and associates somewhere where they can be saved. How difficult could it be, for instance, to take at least one other person with you each time you go to church? The people you take may not always respond to the preacher's invitation, and they may not become a member of the church, but that's not the point. At least you're giving them the opportunity to hear the message of the Gospel.

And you never know what might happen in the future. If you're faithful to plant the seed, others may water it, and it may eventually bring forth fruit. That part is not your responsibility. Just do your part, and God will do His.

Most of us know at least one person whom we consider to be very sincere, and yet they don't know Jesus, so we know that they're sincerely wrong. We carry a burden for them and pray for their salvation, and that's good. But don't fail to tell them the Good News of Jesus and His love.

Too many times we miss the opportunities presented to us to share our faith with others. People who need Christ are right there next to us, and we're talking, and we can feel their pain. That's the time to speak out.

One day, as our family was out driving on a trip, I came to a stop at a stop light. Glancing over at the car next to us, I saw a woman who was in obvious distress. She was rubbing her head and shaking it, and I wondered what she might be going through. It seemed to me that she was in some sort of mental anguish.

In that moment, my heart went out to her. She might not know Jesus, and if the light turned green and she pulled off, what might she suffer as a result? And what might her children suffer with a mother who was so emotionally distressed? I began to intercede for her, asking the Lord to show me if there was any way I could help her.

I had only seconds, so what could I do in a practical sense? In the heavy traffic of that city, I couldn't just jump out of my car and approach her and introduce myself. In that case, my prayer had to suffice, so I lifted that woman up to God and cried out for someone to reach her.

## DID YOU CATCH ANYTHING?

When someone goes fishing, we always ask them the same question: "Did you catch anything?" That's what interests us most. They may have gotten up at four o'clock in the morning, packed the car, and driven to some remote lake, and they may have been there all day long, but where are the fish to show for their efforts? We want to see the results.

Successful fishing demands the right strategy. You have to use the right bait, and you have to fish in the right place, at the right time, and in the right way. And it's the same with soul-winning. Let the Holy Ghost guide you. When He says, "Now's the time," don't hesitate. He knows man's heart, and He'll give you just the right words to say. Open your mouth, and you'll be amazed at what comes out of it.

Later, you may be surprised when someone says to you, "You don't know how much you helped me. I was going through a terrible time, and you seemed to know just what to say." You shouldn't be surprised. Since God knows man's heart, He knows what he needs to hear.

You may think, "Oh, I could never do that," but you can. God wants to use you, and if He thinks you're the best person for the job, who are you to dispute it? If you're in the right place at the right time, then you're God's chosen spokesperson. You may be the only one of God's children present, so don't wait for someone else to do your job.

The Good Samaritan about whom Jesus spoke came to the aid of a man whom others had passed by. Let that Good Samaritan be you. There may be someone lying near you who has been stripped and wounded, and they're half dead. Don't just invite them to church. Give them the Good News. Help them.

With the thousands of church buildings that exist in our cities today, it's a tragedy that most Christians are not telling the very people who need their help that Jesus lives, that He loves them, and that they can be saved. Often, when the Christians go to church themselves, it's just to get their word so that they can make it through the day. They have no time to think of others who are outside the church and so desperately in need.

## JESUS AND ZACCHAEUS

The story of Zacchaeus is one of the most known and beloved of the entire Bible. It is also enlightening on this subject of winning souls:

*Then Jesus entered and passed through Jericho. Now behold, there was a man named Zacchaeus who was a chief tax collector, and he was rich. And He sought to see who Jesus was, but could not because of the crowd, for he was of short stature.*

Luke 19:1-3

This man Zacchaeus was not just anybody; he was a man of prestige and position. As the Chief Tax Collector (perhaps equivalent to the head of the IRS in our country), he was very prosperous— "*rich.*" Still, he didn't know Jesus. So what could his power and his money get him?

Zacchaeus heard about Jesus and wanted to meet Him, so as Jesus was coming into his town one day, he went out to meet Him. The problem was that there was a great crowd about Jesus, and Zacchaeus was very short. Most wealthy and prestigious people would have given up at this point, but not Zacchaeus. He so desperately wanted to see Jesus that he took action:

*So he ran ahead, climbed up into a sycamore tree to see Him, for He was going to pass that way.*

Luke 19:4

Something was obviously driving this man to take rash actions. How would it look for such a wealthy man to run and climb up into a tree to be able to see some man passing by? Well, Zacchaeus didn't really care how it looked. He wanted to see Jesus. All of his money and prestige hadn't satisfied his longing soul. He had to have more, and somehow he felt that Jesus could help him.

He anticipated the route Jesus would take, ran ahead of the crowd, and found a good spot from which he could observe the Master. He was like a visitor to our New Orleans Mardi Gras. He had to find a good spot from which he could see everything. He found just the spot he wanted—up in a tree. From there, he could see everything.

When Jesus came to that place, He stopped, looked up into the tree, and saw Zacchaeus there clinging to a limb for safety. He always sees the hungry hearts. The fact that He saw Zacchaeus is rather amazing because there was a great crowd of people all around Him, pulling on Him, trying to touch Him, asking Him questions, and confiding problems to Him. Still, with all of that confusion and tumult, Jesus had time for Zacchaeus:

*And when Jesus came to the place, He looked up and saw him, and said to him, "Zacchaeus, make haste and come down, for today I must stay at your house."*

Luke 19:5

Zacchaeus didn't even know for sure who Jesus was, but Jesus knew who he was. Jesus also knew where Zacchaeus lived and what he needed. Isn't it interesting that with all of His friends around Him, Jesus had a desire to visit Zacchaeus, to enter his house, and to change his life?

Jesus, of course, wants to be your house guest too, and He loves your neighbor and your friend in this same intimate way. Take Him home with you, and encourage others to do the same.

It isn't enough for us to frequent God's house; He wants to live in our house too. Take Him home with you, and then tell others the Good News. Jesus wants to live in their house too.

Zacchaeus was delighted with Jesus' offer, and he jumped at the chance to host the Lord:

*So he made haste and came down, and received Him joyfully.*

Luke 19:6

Zacchaeus *"made haste"* to receive Jesus, and he *"received Him joyfully,* and we must encourage others to do the same. But not everyone was happy with Jesus' visit to the house of Zacchaeus:

*But when they saw it, they all murmured, saying, "He has gone to be a guest with a man who is a sinner."*

Luke 19:7

There's that old "messed up" mindset again! What is such a good person doing with such a bad person? But remember, again, that you were once among the bad people, and Jesus saved you. If you never reach out to sinners, how can they ever become saints?

Jesus was perfect God, so what was He doing in the house of a sinner? Many could not understand it, but Jesus was doing what He was sent to the earth to do. He didn't come for the righteous, but for those who needed Him. He said:

*Those who are well have no need of a physician, but those who are sick.*

Matthew 9:12

Why then has the Church so isolated itself from the world? It may be that we have done it so that the world will not influence us, but in doing that, we have lost our influence over the world. We encourage new believers not to have fellowship with sinners so that they won't be tempted to slip back into sin themselves. But, in doing so, we have kept them from winning their former intimates in the world.

It's true that some Christians act one way in church and a completely different way outside. That, of course, is wrong, and that's not what we're talking about

126

here. There's nothing wrong with rubbing shoulders with sinners when you know who you are in Christ and you want your experience to rub off on others.

Jesus went to the house of Zacchaeus because He knew that His visit would change Zacchaeus forever, and it did:

*Then Zacchaeus stood and said to the Lord, "Look, Lord, I give half of my goods to the poor; and if I have taken anything from anyone by false accusation, I restore fourfold."*

Luke 19:8

That was exactly the reaction Jesus wanted, and what did He say about it?

*And Jesus said to him, "Today salvation has come to this house, because he also is a son of Abraham; for the Son of Man has come to seek and to save that which was lost."*

Luke 19:9-10

This was His purpose, so how could He not do it? Those self-righteous observers wondered how He could fellowship with sinners, but Jesus wondered how He could not. This was the very reason He had come to earth. Why would He not now fulfill His purpose? And the same is true for each of us.

The church has become a museum of sorts for saints, but God intended it to be a hospital for sinners. It was not intended as a congregation of the perfect, but as a place where the imperfect can go to be perfected. The church is not just a place for "right" people to meet. It's a place for wrong people to get "right." It's not a place for good people to congratulate each other. It's a place for bad people to become good.

Many sinners feel that they have to get their life straightened out before they can begin to frequent the house of God, but that's a mistake. Go to the house of God, and God will help you get your life straightened out. Do we clean fish before we even catch them? That would be impossible.

God invites us to come just as we are. He's not concerned about how well our clothes fit us, or if we have a proper garment to wear. He loves our souls and wants to save us. Those other things can come later.

Some churches forbid entry to those who are improperly dressed. If a lady has pants on that are too tight or she's not fully covered, they don't want her inside their building. But Jesus wants her. Once she is in His care, the Holy Ghost will deal with her, and she'll change the way she dresses.

If you're offended by what someone wears, buy them some new clothes, but don't keep them out of the kingdom because they don't yet know how to dress. What they're currently wearing may be all they have, so if you forbid them entry to the sanctuary as they are, you may be damning their soul to an eternity in hell.

The church was not intended to be some exclusive social club. We were blessed to be a blessing, to share what we have with those who don't yet have it. God is not pleased when we restrict entry to His house. His Word declares:

*And the Spirit and the bride say, "Come!" And let him who hears say, "Come!" And let him who thirsts come. Whoever desires, let him take the water of life freely.*

Revelation 22:17

We don't care what the people who are coming to our church did last year. We don't even care what they did last night. Get them into God's house, and let the Holy Ghost do the rest.

Jesus brought salvation to Zacchaeus, and He wants to do the same thing today for the lost around you. Reaching the lost is the closest thing to His heart.

Everywhere Jesus went, He was doing miracles, so He had a fan club of sorts that followed Him. These fans adored Him and would have done anything at all for Him. Still, He was willing to part from the company of those who loved Him so much to reach out to one who had not yet come to know Him.

The fact that Jesus loved Zacchaeus and brought him salvation had nothing to do with the fact that he was powerful and rich. Jesus cares for the humblest and lowliest of men, and He reaches out to whomever is willing to receive Him.

## WHY ARE YOU STILL HERE ON EARTH?

Think about something for a minute. If God loves you so much (and we know that He does), why has He left you on this wicked and corrupted earth? After you came to know Him and were saved, why did He not take you immediately to be with Him? If your purpose here is only to sing and shout and rejoice in God, you could have done that even better in His presence. You would be so much happier walking on streets of gold today.

God, in His wisdom, has not raptured us out of this world. He has left us here, and therefore He must have a purpose for our lives. It's important that we discover it. The church seems to be just "hanging on," waiting for the Lord to come back, but surely there's more to life than that.

If God's purpose for us was to get deeper in His Word, we could do that so much better sitting at the feet of the apostles in heaven. They wrote the Bible, so they understand it much better than we ever could.

So, why *did* God leave us here? He left us here to glorify Him, to be His representatives on the earth, to speak for Him to men who don't yet know Him. He left us here to honor Him and draw men to Him.

Many of us are well qualified in this area. We've walked through the fires and yet not been burned. We've persevered through demon attacks. We've been miraculously healed from deadly illnesses. Our testimonies are powerful, and the world around us needs to hear them.

Our visits to the church (where we worship together, hear God's Word preached, and pray for one another for personal victory over anything that hinders us) are to prepare us for our greater purpose. That greater purpose is to share our victories with those who have none of their own.

Has your mouth been sealed when it should have been opened? Have you maintained your silence when you should have spoken? This is a serious sin, for someone's deliverance is in your mouth. Somebody is waiting to hear about your experiences. If you're so consumed with your own life that you never take time to tell others, God will not hold you guiltless.

At Beacon Light Cathedral, our goal is to win the lost at any cost. That's the reason we've been crisscrossing the State of Louisiana in recent years, traveling up and down Highway 90, Interstate 10, and Interstate 55, reaching out to men and women in need wherever we could find them. It would be so much easier just to settle down in one place and enjoy life, but there's too much at stake. If God's heart is for the lost, then mine must be too.

Thousands of people attend our services every week in New Orleans, and I could easily be happy with that. But since God isn't, I can't be either.

129

It's been my joy in recent years to be able to pull many young men and women pastors to my side and mentor them. It's not that I have all the answers. I don't. But what a joy it is to pour into these young ones and then see them pouring into others. I release what I have to them, and then I see them releasing it to others. This brings me great joy. In this way, my soul-winning ability is multiplied.

In closing this chapter, let me say that anytime we're not winning the lost, we're not in the perfect will of God. *"Learn to do good"* as it relates to the lost, and in so doing, you will be on your way to *Doing "Right" in a Wrong World.*

# CHAPTER 10

# Being the "Right" Man in the "Right" Place at the "Right" Time

*On the third day there was a wedding in Cana of Galilee, and the mother of Jesus was there. Now both Jesus and His disciples were invited to the wedding. And when they ran out of wine, the mother of Jesus said to Him, "They have no wine."*

*Jesus said to her, "Woman, what does your concern have to do with Me? My hour has not yet come."*

*His mother said to the servants, "Whatever He says to you, do it."*

*Now there were set there six waterpots of stone, according to the manner of purification of the Jews, containing twenty or thirty gallons apiece. Jesus said to them, "Fill the waterpots with water." And they filled them up to the brim."*

John 2:1-7

This is the first in a parade of miracles that can be found within the confines of the Gospel of St. John. John mentions seven different miracles, which he calls "signs." On this first occasion, Jesus turned water into wine at a wedding celebration.

There are still many people alive today who don't believe in miracles. If you were to ask them, "Does God work miracles today?" they wouldn't be able to give you a straight answer. They're not sure. I firmly believe in miracles, and the reason I do is that I am a miracle. Every morning, as I stand in my bathroom and brush my teeth, I find myself staring at a miracle in the mirror. And that miracle stares right back at me.

Our very existence is a miracle, but the greatest miracle is the transformation of a soul. It's when a sinner, through the preached or taught Word, is converted and comes out of the world of darkness, to walk in the marvelous light of Christ. There's no miracle quite like it. To this cause, Jesus gave His life, and He has called us to do the same.

I love the book of John because his tone is a little different from Matthew, Mark, and Luke. These four books—Matthew, Mark, Luke, and John—make up what we call the Synoptic Gospels. They all reveal Jesus, but they reveal Him in different lights. Many times, these gospels offer the same stories, but with different details.

In his narrative, John gets straight to the point and shows us Jesus on the move, making an impact on His world, making a difference in the daily lives of the people with whom He came in contact.

John continued his narrative:

*When the master of the feast had tasted the water that was made wine, and did not know where it came from (but the servants who had drawn the water knew), the master of the feast called the bridegroom. And he said to him, "Every man at the beginning sets out the good wine; and when the guests have well drunk, then the inferior: but you have kept the good wine until now."*

*This beginning of signs Jesus did in Cana of Galilee, and manifested His glory; and His disciples believed in Him."*

John 2:9-11

This was just the beginning of the many "signs" that Jesus would do.


## WHAT IS A SIGN?

What is a "sign"? A sign is a miracle with a message. Every miracle that Jesus did had a message attached to it. Every sign had a significance.

And what was the purpose of these "signs," these miracles? God tells us in the final chapter of the book of John:

*And truly Jesus did many other signs in the presence of His disciples, which are not written in this book. But these are written, that you may believe that Jesus is the Christ, the Son of God, and that believing you may have life in His name.*

John 20:30-31

Not every miracle Jesus did was recorded, but those that were recorded were recorded for a reason—so that we might believe. There are three things I want you to see about this first miracle that Jesus did. The first important thing was the setting of the miracle.

## THE SETTING OF THE MIRACLE

The setting for this miracle was a wedding. A wedding is always a happy occasion in the community, and it's clear that Jesus always attended them (as well as funerals). Although He never broke up a wedding feast, He was known to break up funerals (by raising the dead).

The point is that Jesus didn't live aloof from everyone else. He made Himself one of the people, one of the everyday common men in His community. He was not always in the synagogue teaching and preaching, as some might imagine. He went places, and He did things. He lived life to the fullest and enjoyed every minute of it.

Jesus didn't go to this particular wedding to make a point, and He didn't force His way into it to teach the people a lesson. He went because He was invited to go, and the same was true of His disciples. Jesus always accepts an invitation, and if you invite Him, He'll be present at your social occasions too. And when He's present, He'll add something to your life. That's what Jesus does; He adds meaning to our existence.

A small boy was beginning to study mathematics in school. The next Sunday, sitting next to his mother in church, he noticed what looked to him like a mathematical symbol on the communion table. "Mama," he whispered "why is there a plus sign on the communion table?"

Startled, the mother had to look to see what he was talking about. "That's not a plus sign," she whispered back. "That's the cross." But I think the child had a revelation. The cross adds to our lives, and Jesus had come to the wedding that day to add something that was missing.

It seems significant to me that the Bible failed to mention the name of either the bride or the groom, the most important individuals at the wedding that day. The bride and groom are always the center of attention at any wedding.

There could be several explanations for this oversight, but I'm convinced that it was because these were common people, not extremely significant in the view of others. Because He was there, of course, Jesus became the center of attention at this particular wedding.

These were just ordinary people, not big shots. They were people with no name, no title, and no particular fame, but they invited Jesus, and He came. There's a powerful message in that fact. Jesus doesn't care who you are. If you invite Him, He'll show up at your house and attend your party.

There was a problem at this wedding, a lack, a need. They ran out of wine. This is another indication to us of the lowly estate of the families involved.

The mother of Jesus pointed out the problem to Him, and like most sons, He had a not-so-pleasant response for her. Was He suddenly the wedding coordinator? He had just come to have a good time, and He was relaxing and enjoying Himself. He hadn't been invited to meddle in the intricate inner workings of the affair. He was just one of the guests. What did Mary expect from Him?

There was a further element to Jesus' question. It wasn't His time yet: *"My hour has not yet come."* By this, He meant that He had not yet begun to manifest His power in the earth. But Mary sensed that it *was* His time, and she gave the servants that amazing instruction: *"Whatever He says to you, do it."*

Mary knew something that Jesus hadn't revealed to anyone else as yet. When there was a problem, He could solve it. How she knew this, we can only imagine. Had He done things as He was growing up to demonstrate this power? Or did she know it by the Spirit? We cannot say for sure.

Whatever the case, the words that came from Mary that day are among the wisest recorded anywhere. *"Whatever He says to you, do it."* Those are still wise words today in the twenty-first century.

The next thing we know, Jesus, the Lord of Glory, was taking care of the refreshments at a wedding party. This indicates to us that He wants to be with us and to help us, not just on Sunday mornings, or at some other time when we're in His house. He wants to be with us at every critical moment of our lives, and He wants to help us with the smallest detail of our everyday life.

*Jesus has a way of turning the monotonous into something monumental...*

He'll be with you on Wednesday morning in the office, just as He is on Sunday morning at the church you attend, but He's awaiting your invitation. Sure, you take Him to church with you, but do you invite Him into the other parts of your life?

He knows when things have happened to aggravate you, and He wants to be there to help you. Do you invite Him? Do you invite His presence on Friday evening, just as you do on Sunday morning? He's interested in every single one of us, every single day of our lives, and with every single circumstance that we encounter along life's way.

We owe it to ourselves to invite Him to join us. His presence at the wedding that day turned what could have been a disaster into something absolutely delightful. And He's ready to do the very same thing for you and me.

Can you imagine how embarrassed the bride and groom and their parents would have been if they had run out of wine at the reception and had no way of getting more? I can just imagine the turmoil the bride would have experienced. She might even have gotten angry with her groom and said, "How will you take care of me when you can't even keep the refreshments flowing at our wedding feast?" This was not just a physical disaster; it had the potential for an emotional and relational disaster as well. This otherwise loving couple might never have recovered from such an embarrassment.

Jesus has a way of turning the monotonous into something monumental, and He was about to bring joy and happiness back into this devastating situation. When the miracle came, it would come through obedience: *"Whatever He says to you, do it."*

How Jesus did this miracle is interesting. He spotted some large stone waterpots sitting there. They could hold some twenty to thirty gallons each. *"Fill the waterpots with water,"* He told the servants.

135

These were good servants. When Mary said, *"Whatever He says to you, do it,"* they listened. Now, when Jesus told them to fill the waterpots with water, *"they filled them up to the brim."* That's obedience, and God honors it every time.

You may not realize what God is about to do in your life. If you did, it would put a smile on your face. He can turn your devastating situation into something delightful. Things may look bad for you right now, but when you invite Jesus into the situation, He'll make all the difference.

## THE SYMBOLISM OF THE MIRACLE

The second thing I want to point out in this story is the symbolism attached to the miracle. After the servants had obediently filled the waterpots with water, Jesus next told them to take some of it out and carry it to the master of the feast for his approval. They began to do this.

Apparently, that's when the miracle took place. As the servants dipped the water out of the jars, it was no longer water. It was now wine. They had done what they could do, *"they took it"* (John 2:8), and Jesus did the rest.

Let's look one more time at what happened next:

*When the master of the feast had tasted the water that was made wine, and did not know where this wine came from (but the servants who had drawn the water knew), the master of the feast called the bridegroom.*

John 2:9

*"The servants knew."* They knew because they had drawn the water. They knew because they had been obedient. The master of the feast didn't know, but the servants knew. Are you a servant?

If you want to be on the inside spiritually, having the inside scoop on what God is doing these days, become a servant. His Word declares:

*Surely the Lord God does nothing, unless He reveals His secrets to His servants the prophets.*

Amos 3:7

Servants know secrets.

The servants in the White House know something about our president that most of the rest of us don't know. The servants in the governors' mansions around our country see things behind the scenes that other people are not able to see. The servants in a particular house know things about the activities in that house that not even the closest neighbors may know. Servants are on the inside, and they know what's going on.

The master of the feast immediately called the bridegroom. "Hold up! Hold up, man!" he said. "You've got me confused." What seemed confusing to him was that traditionally people brought out the best wine first and later served something inferior. This groom had done just the opposite. He had saved the best wine until the last.

"Whoa!" he must have said. "I've never tasted a Merlot this good. (I've never had any Zinfandel like this one. Where did you get this Chardonnay?) It's the best I've ever had."

Some of us know more about wines than others. This man knew wines, and he knew that this was the best wine he'd ever tasted.

"I thought we had run out of wine, and suddenly you bring out the very best. What's going on here? You've got things backwards."

I never deal with the issue of whether the wine in question was fermented or not. What is clear is that this story is not about intoxication. We all know that intoxication is Satan's substitute for Jesus' joy.

Too many people, when they have no joy, resort to a bottle. Others do it to forget or to salve their conscience. When they come down and their intoxication has ended, they not only have the same problems still facing them, but they also have a terrible hangover.

Get Jesus' joy on the inside of you, and even though you have problems, even though you must face unpleasant situations, you'll have the assurance that somehow, some way, God will work it all out.

This is a joy that the world can't give and the world can't take away. When you get the real joy of Jesus, you won't need crack cocaine or some other substance to pump you up. Just thinking about the goodness of Jesus and what He's done for you will do it.

You can get high on Jesus and not even have to spend any money doing it. Just remembering the times God has spared your life in the past will give you determination to make it through any difficult days ahead. This is the new wine, and it's the very best.

This world will let you down every time, and what you expected to be endless joy and happiness will invariably run out. That's when Jesus loves to step in, and He'll give you the best.

There were six stone waterpots, and six is the number of man. These waterpots didn't just happen; they were man-made. Still, Jesus decided to use them and ordered them to be filled to the brim. In the same way, He uses us, earthen vessels, to bless others.

Although He uses earthen vessels, He wants them filled to the brim. It's not enough to have Jesus in our lives all mixed up with other elements. We're not to be filled with Jesus and something else, only with Jesus.

Jesus often has to share billing with a spouse, a job, a child, or money. He wants to fill us until there's no room for anyone or anything else in our hearts. All you need is Jesus, and if you're filled up with Him, He'll bring you the spouse or job or money you need. He said:

*But seek first the kingdom of God and His righteousness, and all these things shall be added to you.*

Matthew 6:33

These stone jars were filled to the brim, and you need to be filled to the brim too. Lay hands on yourself today and say, "Fill me up, Lord." You need to be filled to the brim so that you can deal with demons, difficult situations, and difficult people.

## THE SECRET OF THE MIRACLE

There's a secret hidden in verse 5 of our text. Let's look at it once again:

*His mother said to the servants, "Whatever He says to you, do it."*

John 2:5

Why did May say this? Because this is the secret behind every miracle, and if you need a miracle today, you, too, must recognize this fact. Since Jesus is the Source of every miracle, obedience to Him is the key to every miracle.

Before we close this chapter, let's examine the reason God does miracles for us. There are three reasons.

The first reason Jesus did this miracle was for the benefit of the bride and groom. These people needed wine, and so Jesus provided that wine. If another family had a different need, then that's what He did for them. He delights in blessing us where we need Him the most.

The second reason Jesus did this miracle was for their gladness. The lack that had arisen detracted from the usual joy of the wedding reception, and Jesus restored that joy. He delights in seeing His children happy.

The final reason Jesus did the miracle was for His own glory. All three of these reasons are true of the miracle God is about to do for you. It will be for your benefit and the benefit of those around you. It will restore joy to your life and to many others as well, and it will honor God. Be sure that He receives all the glory.

As the master of the feast cast about for an explanation about the origins of the wine he was tasting, the servants must have stood back with big smiles on their faces. The important issue wasn't so much from where the wine had come, but from Whom. Jesus is the Source of all good things.

There are many wonderful lessons to be learned from this simple story:

1. You may not be well known, but that doesn't matter. If you need a miracle, Jesus is interested and concerned.

2. God wants to be with you in your house and on your job. He wants to multiply whatever is in short supply in your life to make it meet your need.

3. No situation is too difficult for Jesus. This situation looked utterly hopeless, but Mary knew that Jesus could handle the problem. And He did.

4. God saves the best until last. Some of you have been very concerned because it seems that others are receiving their miracle, and you're not. But when you're working with Him, He always saves the best for last. Start praising Him because when praises go up, blessings come down. You don't have to wait until the battle is over. You can shout right now. The devil may hit you high and he may hit you low, but he can't steal your joy.

5. The most important lesson of all is that just as Jesus was the "right" man in the "right" place at the "right" time, you can be too. Change the lives of those around you by allowing the Miracle Worker to do His work through you. Personally, I no longer want to be just a "good"

preacher; I want to be the "right" preacher for the moment, the man with God's message of the hour. How about you?

As you're able to take this step, you're well on your way to *Doing "Right" in a Wrong World.*

# CHAPTER 11

# "Right" Living Demands "Right" Giving

*Now the multitude of those who believed were of one heart and one soul; neither did anyone say that any of the things he possessed was his own, but they had all things in common. And with great power the apostles gave witness to the resurrection of the Lord Jesus. And great grace was upon them all. Nor was there anyone among them who lacked.*

Acts 4:32-34

"**N**or *was there anyone among them who lacked.*" What a powerful testimony! How can we achieve that same thing?

As Christians, we have learned the importance of giving offerings to God, but are we giving the "right" offerings. This is important because for many of us, financial problems are our *only* problems. The many things that bring stress to our daily lives are somehow related to financial need.

The arrival of the twenty-first century has brought about a new urgency for us, as Christians, to understand the role the Church is to play in our society as a whole and how it is to impact the world around us. God looks upon society, not as it is, but as He wills it to become. And the Church, individually and corporately, must quickly prepare to meet the challenges of the twenty-first century.

One of the ways we can do that is to free ourselves from the financial mechanisms of the world. Destiny is in our hands, for destiny is not by chance. It's by choice. In this season, you and I must make wise and sound choices.

Good choices will move you toward your destiny. Bad choices will not only add stress to your life; they will actually keep you from your destiny.

This is true especially in the financial realm. When you make poor financial decisions, the resultant fallout holds you back from making progress in life. Some of us are still out of control with our spending and cannot distinguish between a need and a desire. In school, we learned how to count money, but no school can teach you how to manage money. We have a lot to learn.

## WHAT ACTS TEACHES US ABOUT GIVING

The Acts of the Apostles is more than a history book. It's also a model, a paradigm of what the Church of the Lord Jesus should be in the twenty-first century. If you have become comfortable with living from paycheck to paycheck and think that a constant financial struggle is an acceptable way to live, I pray that God's Word may convince you otherwise.

I trust that the Word of God can make you uncomfortable enough with the status quo that you change your thinking about giving.

In Acts 4, the early disciples were blessed financially because they *"were of one heart and one soul."* This unity of spirit was not just evident in matters of worship and community service, but it extended to their financial situations.

Not one person among the group claimed that their belongings were strictly for their personal use. Instead, they were willing to share what they had with others. *"They had all things in common."* In other words, this was their mindset: If I have it and you don't, what's mine is yours too.

The results of this phenomenon were both spiritual and physical. They were blessed spiritually: *"And with great power the apostles gave witness to the resurrection of the Lord Jesus. And great grace was upon them all"* (Acts 4:33). They *"all"* experienced *"great power"* and *"great grace."* And just to remind you, grace is the unmerited favor of God. We don't deserve it, but we receive it anyway.

The early disciples of Christ were also blessed physically: *"Nor was there anyone among them who lacked"* (Acts 4:34). Again, what a great testimony that was! Not one person among them lacked. Not one!

And how was that possible? Believe it or not, it came about through giving:

> *For all who were possessors of lands or houses sold them, and brought the proceeds of the things that were sold, and laid them at the apostles' feet; and they distributed to each as anyone had need.*
>
> Acts 4:34-35

The people were faithful to give, and the apostles used the funds to help those who were in need.

One of the givers among those early Christians was a man named Barnabas. Barnabas would later accompany Paul on some of his missionary journeys. Here's what the Bible had to say about him and his giving:

> *And Joses, who was also named Barnabas by the apostles (which is translated Son of Encouragement), a Levite of the country of Cyprus, having land, sold it, and brought the money and laid it at the apostles' feet.*
>
> Acts 4:36-37

But Barnabas was just one example. It took many working together to make it happen. The first step we need to take toward this type of miraculous provision is for all of us to become one. When we hear about the needs of others, it should move us. This has nothing to do with race or nationality. If someone is in the family, we want to feel their pain.

Here at Beacon Light Cathedral, our goal is to build a financial infrastructure that is based on the Word of God. This must be a financial system that will give us sufficiency, independence, and control over our own affairs, so that we will no longer have to depend on the world around us for our sustenance.

There are business owners in our congregation, for instance, who should never have to go out and look for customers. Our church members should become patrons of those believers who are in business. In this way, we need to cover each other.

What is the goal in all of this? That none suffer lack. Can you imagine what rejoicing there would be in our churches if every single member of the congregation had their financial needs met? How would our people act if they had no bills at all to pay? I can imagine that not one person would be sitting with their arms crossed and their glasses down on the end of their nose. They would be giving God what I call a "crazy praise." And what we need to do is to praise Him like that now, like the need has already been met. Then He will supply it.

God is about to channel some supernatural resources into our lives. Some of you who are reading this book will soon be receiving checks you were not expecting. God is about to give some of you jobs you don't seem to be totally qualified for. Your increase is coming. And when your increase comes, don't forget to be generous.

Most of us have had the experience of someone in need coming to us for help, and we were able to help them. And what we can say about that experience is that it was a wonderful feeling and nothing can compare to it. There's no greater joy in life than being able to bless others. If we have learned to give when we didn't have much, we will be even better givers in the future, as we have more.

But in this matter, the devil will fight you with all he's worth. He doesn't want you to be obedient to God. He wants to keep you in poverty. He knows that when you get to the top, you'll reach down and pull many other people up with you. It never pays to be selfish because God wants to bless us.

## THE IMPORTANCE OF THE TITHE

It's sobering to consider the fact that the state of our finances often reflects the status of our spiritual pilgrimage. You're no further along with God than the point to which you have come to trust Him with your tithe. This has nothing to do with how often you attend church services, but it has everything to do with how much you trust God with the ten percent of your income He has designated as actually belonging to Him.

This one area is responsible for many of your unresolved conflicts, and it could be the reason you still have many unmet needs, the reason you can't ever seem to get ahead, and the reason you continue to live in financial frustration. If we are in direct violation of God's Word, what can you expect? God is bound by His Word, so that what He can and cannot do is defined by that Word and by our obedience (or lack of obedience) to it.

The tithe is the area where many Christians go astray. In some cases, this is because people have not been taught the truth concerning spiritual stewardship or have failed to study it on their own. In other cases, people deliberately disobey God's Word. Surprisingly, some who profess to love God and to love His Word still ignore its clear teachings on this subject.

## GOD'S DESIRE FOR YOU

God wants you to be blessed more than you want to be blessed, and you'd better believe that. How can I be so sure of that? Because He said so. He shows us in His Word that He takes pleasure in the prosperity of His children:

*Beloved, I pray that you may prosper in all things and be in health, just as your soul prospers.*

3 John 1:2

Think about how good it makes you feel to have a child who is successful, who excels at anything in life, who does well. Well, if that makes you feel that good and get that excited, how much more does God feel when we, His children, are doing well?

When God looks down over the banisters of heaven and hears you testifying about His goodness in your life, it's His greatest joy. He wants to bless you more so that you can tell others on your job, in your school, and in your home about it. Your testimony brings Him glory more than anything else.

He wants you to have a new car, a new house, and everything else you need because He knows that when you get it, you'll give Him glory for it. Then you and He both will look good. So He wants you blessed.

So what is it that's holding many of us back? Let's see what God has to say about it in His Word?

*"For I am the LORD, I do not change; therefore you are not consumed, O sons of Jacob. Yet from the days of your fathers you have gone away from My ordinances and have not kept them. Return to Me, and I will return to you," says the LORD of hosts. "But you said, 'In what way shall we return?' Will a man rob God? Yet you have robbed Me! But you say, 'In what way have we robbed You?' In tithes and offerings. You are cursed with a curse, for you have robbed Me, even this whole nation. Bring all*

*the tithes into the storehouse, that there may be food in My house, and try Me now in this," says the LORD of hosts, "If I will not open for you the windows of heaven and pour out for you such blessing that there will not be room enough to receive it."*

Malachi 3:6-10

I would be an absolute fool to teach this to my people and not live it myself. I became a tither in November of 1986, and I've been tithing faithfully ever since. And since that time, the blessings of God have come upon my life in ever greater measure.

The secret of tithing is to learn to trust God in the little and in the much. But it begins with the little. If you can be faithful to tithe from an income of seventy dollars a week, then God knows that you'll be faithful to tithe if He gives you seven hundred dollars a week. Some want to move on to seven thousand dollars a week, but because they haven't yet learned how to be faithful with the seventy dollars a week, God can't trust them with any more.

When you have more money, it makes you a bigger whatever you already are, so if you're already a giver, having more money will make you a bigger giver. But if you're robbing God, having more money will just make you a bigger thief.

The Lord began this teaching on tithing by saying that He does not change. Thank God for that. We're only here because of His mercy and grace. If we had received what was due us, we would have been consumed long ago by His anger.

Still, despite the fact of God's amazing grace and mercy toward us, many people are slow to be obedient to Him, and one of the areas in which He demands obedience is with the tithe. He calls men who fail to pay it robbers and declares that they're cursed. This is serious, and we need to see what God is saying and why.

## GOD'S APPARENT PROBLEM WITH US

For some of you, God loves you, but He has a problem with you. He's keeping you and protecting you and providing for your sustenance, but He's not happy with you. Oh, He's not about to kick you out of His house, and He's not about to disown you as a child. But, at the same time, He's not pleased with your progress either. You're like a disobedient child that brings anguish to the entire family.

When a child comes home with a bad report card, we don't shut them out of the house, but we do feel that somehow we have to express our displeasure. We cannot refuse to allow them to come to the table and eat, but there are ways that we can show them how hurt we are and how strongly we feel that their behavior is unacceptable and has to change. To say the least, we're very disappointed.

We perhaps had in our minds to buy them a special gift, but this delays it indefinitely. It may come in time, but at the moment, that remains to be seen.

I'm afraid that is exactly what has happened to many believers. They should have had blessings long ago, but those blessings were delayed by their disobedience, while God expressed His displeasure and showed them that their behavior needed to change. *"You have gone away from My ordinances and have not kept them,"* God says, and He simply cannot let that pass.

So what is the solution? *" 'Return to Me, and I will return to you,' says the LORD of hosts."* It is you who has caused the problem, and it is you who must resolve it. God hasn't done anything bad; you have. God is ready to bless you— just as soon as you return to His good graces through obedience.

Is there something specific we have done, and something specific we can do to make amends? Yes, God shows us. We have robbed Him, and if we'll stop robbing Him, His blessing will return to us.

How have we robbed God? *"In tithes and offerings."* And when you do that, you bring a curse upon yourself. No one has cursed you; you have cursed yourself.

It's time to lift the curse, and only you can do it. This is a personal problem. You created it, and only you can resolve it. Look again at what God said and notice this time the personal aspect of it I have emphasized here:

*"Yet from the days of YOUR fathers YOU have gone away from My ordinances and have not kept them. Return to Me, and I will return to YOU," says the Lord of hosts. "But YOU said, 'In what way shall we return?' Will a man rob God? Yet YOU have robbed Me! But YOU say, 'In what way have we robbed You?' In tithes and offerings. YOU are cursed with a curse, for YOU have robbed Me, even this whole nation. Bring all the tithes into the storehouse, that there may be food in My house, and try Me now in this," says the Lord of hosts, "If I will not open for YOU the windows of heaven*

*and pour out for YOU such blessing that there will not be room enough to receive it."*

Malachi 3:6-10

If you're ready to return to Him, then He's ready to return to you. But what is the point of return?

The point of return is always the point of departure. When you ask God, "Where do I start getting back to Your blessing?" He will answer, "At the same point where you started losing it." The place to get it right is the same place you started getting it wrong. Get back on right at the same point where you got off. Come back in the same door you left from. And, for many, this is in the area of tithes and offerings.

Have you been giving what many might consider "good" offerings, but which you know in your heart are not the "right" offerings? Then that's your problem. That why you're experiencing lack.

Faithful tithing will do a lot more than bring money to you. It will help your children improve their grades in school. It will add years to your life and to the things you own. Things that should be worn out by now will keep working long after you expect them to quit. It will keep your car running well and your roof from leaking. It will keep you well and strong.

God wants to do all of that and more for us, but He has an apparent problem with us. His problem is that we're not willing to do even the minimum that He has required of us as proof of our love and devotion.

## GOD'S APPOINTED PROGRAM FOR US

God has an apparent problem with us, but He doesn't intend to leave us there under a curse. He has a plan to set us free and put us on the road to prosperity.

God is saying to you today, "I want to give you more, but I also want you to do better in your obedience to Me." Some of us know just how God feels. If our children obey us two times out of five, they think they've done something great. We want to do something for them, but we can't do it until they show us that they can assume responsibility.

There are many things that God wants to place into our lives, but when we can't even get up on time and get ready to go on time, what can He do? His hands are tied. Those hands are literally full of blessings for us, but we're holding them back and preventing God from opening them up to us.

You think that God has to work to get your miracle ready for you, but it's just the opposite. He has to get you ready for your miracle. If He could get five days of consistent obedience out of you, He could do amazing things. The blessing is ready, and has been ready for some time, but you're still not yet ready for it.

*Give God a try. See if He won't open the windows of heaven over your life.*

Here's God's program:

*Bring all the tithes into the storehouse, that there may be food in My house, and try Me now in this," says the Lord of hosts, "if I will not open for you the windows of heaven and pour out for you such blessing that there will not be room enough to receive it.*

Malachi 3:10

Give God a try. See if He won't open the windows of heaven over your life.

He has made some amazing promises to those who tithe. He will pour out on them such blessings that they won't have room to receive them. He will also rebuke the devourer for their sakes.

Many of us know what the work of *"the devourer"* is. The minute we start getting ahead, he comes to eat up our increase and put us back in the hole.

Farmers and fruit growers know about devourers and the terrible destruction they can bring. You can wait all year on a crop of apples to ripen, but if they turn out to be full of worms, all is lost. You have a harvest of sorts, but you can't appreciate it, and it does you very little good.

You have an income, but something happens to deplete that income and make your life miserable. This is complicated by our selfish spending that drives us into needless and foolish debt. We're like little children saying, "Lord, give me more." But He's saying, "Why should I increase you, when you're not being faithful with what you already have."

He has a program for your recovery, but that program requires that you get it "right." It's not enough to give a "good" offering. You have to give the "right" offering. If God has blessed you with one hundred and eighty dollars, then you owe Him eighteen dollars. That's more than fair. And if you will do your part, you'll be amazed by what God does. He will open the windows of heaven over your life.

If we have indeed been guilty of robbing God, then the remedy is to enter His rehabilitation program. Obey Him, and He will bless you.

Some seem to foolishly expect God not to notice when they've robbed Him. Who are we kidding? Can we pull the wool over God's eyes? Can we rob Him and not be identified as the guilty party? Stop fooling yourself. If you're guilty, He knows it, and there is no escaping that fact.

He knows what your paycheck is even before you receive it. He knew what it was before taxes were taken out, and He knows what it is after the taxes have been taken out. You can't fool Him.

And all He's asking for is ten percent. That's all. In return, He has promised to send angels to watch over you and all that is yours.

This is not complicated. If you have four hundred dollars, God wants you to give Him forty of it. What's complicated about that? This is as simple as it could possibly be.

And, if we do this simplest thing, then God will open the windows of heaven over us. He will stretch the ninety percent we have left over and make it go further. He will put it in the hearts of other people to bless us, and we'll not even know why they're blessing us.

## GOD'S ABUNDANT PROVISION FOR US

If we can just become willing to prove God in this simple way, He has promised that He will pour us out so many blessings that we won't have room enough to contain them. These are not all financial blessings. Tithing will bring healing to your relationships, make your marriage stronger, cause your stress level to decrease, and many other wonderful things.

This promise of provision for our lives through tithing involves both quality and quantity. God wants you to enjoy both.

Some of us had better learn to tithe because we have expensive tastes. We don't like cheap "stuff." We're attracted to things of quality. And God is not offended by that. He likes it.

If you're a child of God, there's no reason in the world that you can't drive a nice car. You should own a nice home. God doesn't have a problem with that.

Every year "Forbes" magazine releases its list of the richest people in America. As usual, this past year, it was Bill Gates, founder of Microsoft Corporation. He was worth $46 billion at that point. At the very end of the list (which included four hundred very wealthy people) was Tereza Heinze Kerry, wife of unsuccessful Democratic candidate for the presidency, John Kerry. She was worth a mere $750 million.

Most of us would love to be somewhere at the bottom of that list. I wouldn't mind being number four hundred and one myself. But what's my point? God has said: *"The wealth of the sinner is stored up for the righteous"* (Proverbs 13:22).

When is the moment when that promise will become reality? It's getting closer all the time. God is about to kiss us with unusual favor. He's about to put us in a position that men will not be able to say no to us. Because of our faithfulness, He will open the windows of heaven over us. He will bless us, He will bless our children, and He will bless everything that pertains to us.

If you have passed the test, if you have proven God, get ready for the release of favor. Your time of struggle is coming to an end, and God is positioning you for great favor. Get ready to be blessed as never before.

When God first gave me this message, in the fall of 2004, I was on a flight from Houston to Raleigh-Durham, North Carolina. God showed me that we needed to set a test period in which we could prove Him and His promises.

Since we had just ninety days left in the year, I set a period of ninety days as the test. Within that period we needed to make a special sacrificial offering to His work, and within that period, we would see His hand at work in our lives.

When I got back to New Orleans, I challenged our people to believe God to be more productive in the last ninety days of the year than they had been in the first nine months of it. God could do that for us miraculously through our obedience in giving. And I challenged them to sow a seed faith offering of a dollar a day for the remaining ninety days in the year.

I knew that not everyone would hear this message, but God showed me that there would be a remnant of those who would hear His voice and obey. And blessing would come because of it.

It didn't matter that many had been going through some terrible challenges all year. God showed me that they could have a strong finish to the year through obedience to Him in this matter. And, of course, He didn't fail us.

Those who learn to give to God never lose, and learning this secret will bring you one step closer to *Doing "Right" in a Wrong World.*

# CHAPTER 12

# "Right" Living Demands the "Right" Kind of Stewardship

*Then the Pharisees went and plotted how they might entangle Him in His talk. And they sent to Him their disciples with the Herodians, saying, "Teacher, we know that You are true, and teach the way of God in truth; nor do You care about anyone, for You do not regard the person of men. Tell us, therefore, what do You think? Is it lawful to pay taxes to Caesar, or not?"*

*But Jesus perceived their wickedness, and said, "Why do you test Me, you hypocrites? Show Me the tax money."*

*So they brought Him a denarius.*

*And He said to them, "Whose image and inscription is this?"*

*They said to Him, "Caesar's."*

*And He said to them, "Render therefore to Caesar the things that are Caesar's, and to God the things that are God's."*

Matthew 22:15-21

There is no subject in the Bible upon which Jesus lavished more time than that of stewardship. Still, I know people who have been faithfully attending church for fifteen years or more and yet have not embraced the truth of God's Word on this matter. As we noted previously, they claim to love the Bible and to take it as their rule of faith, and yet they blatantly continue to disregard its imperatives on this issue.

God loves us so much that He will never force us to obey Him. What great love!

Tithing and tithing alone will never get you out of debt. It will never blanket you from financial challenge. Tithing is just the floor where we begin, not the ceiling where we end. There is much more to learn about "right" stewardship.

The devil is not intimidated by the average Christian because he knows that they're Christians in word only, and not in their actions. At this late date in the game, we're still struggling to get God's people to tithe faithfully. In the average church here in America, fully eighty percent of the members do not yet tithe. That's scandalous.

Eight out of ten professing Christians rob God. And they don't just do it one time. They do it week after week, month after month, and year after year.

This race is being run, and we're still trying get people to the starting line. How crazy is that? This is the last thing we should be struggling with right now. Giving God a dime out of every dollar to prove our love and faithfulness should have been settled long ago.

If God can't trust us with the smallest things, how can He trust us with *"true riches"* (Luke 16:11)? If God can't trust you with quarters and one-dollar bills, how can He trust you with larger amounts?

And what are these *"true riches"* that many are still living without? What might be ours we can often only imagine. I'm convinced that one of the *"true riches"* of which the Lord spoke here was His favor. When God's favor is upon you, the actions, attitudes, or abilities of other men will be used to enrich your life. That's something we could all use.

## RENDERING TO CAESAR WHAT IS CAESAR'S

When the Pharisees came to Jesus on this occasion, trying to find something against Him, He knew what was in their hearts. Still, He didn't refuse to speak with them.

When they asked Him if they should pay taxes to the Roman government of the day, He asked to see a coin. Noting Caesar's inscription on it, He asked them to identify it. When they said it was Caesar's, He told them to render to Caesar what was Caesar's and to God what was His.

Some Christians would never consider cheating on their taxes or not paying them altogether, and yet they dare to rob God. What are they thinking?

When you go to a store to buy something, they give you one price before taxes and another price after taxes. The amount of tax varies around the country and the world, but here in Louisiana we pay nine percent sales tax on most items we purchase. That's just part of the purchase. The government gets it share of every sale.

You could never say to a sales clerk: "Well, I'll pay you for the item, but not for the tax on it." You don't have that alternative, and they don't have the right to sell you the item that way. The government will get its due one way or another.

So this is not a voluntary giving. The system demands it and takes it from us—whether we like it or not.

We not only pay sales taxes; we pay property taxes, income taxes, unemployment taxes, and many other kinds of taxes. Many of these taxes are hidden in our telephone bills and other monthly expenses. We don't like it sometimes, but we understand it. The government has to get its money somehow for the many programs it administers. So we pay our taxes, rendering unto Caesar what is his. Still, because we're not forced to do so, we sometimes fail to render to God what is rightfully His, and we use every imaginable argument to justify our actions.

## THE ORIGIN OF THE TITHE

As we noted in the last chapter, God wants you blessed more than you even want to be blessed, and the tithe is the starting place for God to get involved in your personal affairs. Still, I've heard some people claim that the tithe is nothing more than a carryover from the Old Testament and that it's not applicable for this dispensation of grace. But the tithe existed among the people of God long before the Law itself came into existence:

*Then Melchizedek king of Salem brought out bread and wine; he was the priest of God Most High. And he blessed him and said:*

155

*"Blessed be Abram of God Most High, Possessor of heaven and earth; and blessed be God Most High, Who has delivered your enemies into your hand." And he gave him a tithe of all.*

Genesis 14:18-20

The Law would not come for many more generations, and already men were paying their tithes to God through His servants. So don't allow the enemy to trick you into not tithing. This is your way out of trouble.

Some of you have finances that are so "messed up" that you don't know which way is up, and you need divine intervention. With the bills you currently have and the income you currently have, there's no way you can make it otherwise. The numbers just don't add up. You need a miracle from God.

Some pastors are afraid to teach on tithing for fear their members will think they only want money. But this subject doesn't intimidate me because I've learned to walk in it. I've proven it in my own life, and I know that it works. I'm a living example of the benefits of this teaching, the fruit of faithful tithing.

When you connect with God in this area, you'll see what a difference His favor on your life makes too.

## WHY WAS ABRAHAM SO BLESSED?

Why was Abraham so blessed? Why did he have herds of animals, and gold and silver, and other forms of wealth? Because he was faithful to tithe to God. This tradition of tithing was carried on by Abraham's descendants, among them, his grandson Jacob:

*And he called the name of that place Bethel; but the name of that city had been Luz previously. Then Jacob made a vow, saying, "If God will be with me, and keep me in this way that I am going, and give me bread to eat and clothing to put on, so that I come back to my father's house in peace, then the Lord shall be my God. And this stone which I have set as a pillar shall be God's house, and of all that You give me I will surely give a tenth to You."*

Genesis 28:19-22

Jacob made a vow to God. If God would take care of Him, he would tithe. *"Of all that You give me I will surely give a tenth to You."* This should have been

156

what we call a "no-brainer" for Jacob. After all, God has promised to bless us, to entrust to us, if you will, great riches, and the only thing He requires in return is that we recognize the Source of our blessing by returning to Him a small portion, ten percent. As I noted before, that's not too difficult.

God doesn't take His portion by force. He will not twist your arm to take it from you. And He will not remove it from your check before you get it (like Uncle Sam does). God's portion is strictly voluntary. He wants us to willingly and joyfully decide to honor Him as our Source by giving the first ten percent of our increase to Him.

If the tithe is to be paid, it must be done of your own volition and free will. It will not be by force. If you don't pay it, it won't be paid.

But it's dangerous to touch something as holy as the tithe that God has set aside for Himself and His servants:

## THE TITHE IS HOLY

*"And all the tithe of the land, whether of the seed of the land or of the fruit of the tree, is the Lord's. It is holy to the Lord. If a man wants at all to redeem any of his tithes, he shall add one-fifth to it. And concerning the tithe of the herd or the flock, of whatever passes under the rod, the tenth one shall be holy to the Lord. He shall not inquire whether it is good or bad, nor shall he exchange it; and if he exchanges it at all, then both it and the one exchanged for it shall be holy; it shall not be redeemed."*

*These are the commandments which the Lord commanded Moses for the children of Israel on Mount Sinai.*

Leviticus 27:30-34

The tithe is holy. That means that God has separated it unto Himself. One tenth of our income does not belong to us; it's God's. If it comes down to paying your tithe and honoring other commitments, by all means pay your tithe first. If it comes down to paying your tithe or doing something special for your pastor, obey God in the tithe, and God will take care of your pastor.

If God's tithe is on your back in the form of a new dress or a new suit, you're in trouble. That tithe is holy. Don't use it for any other purpose.

God's tithe invested into your home can never result in blessings for you and your family. The tithe is not to be spent on video games, some new electronic gadget, or a new High Definition television set.

Don't be guilty of driving the Lord's holy tithe down the street. That's too dangerous for words. The Lord's holy tithe is also not to be invested in some stock, bond, or savings account. You will not be blessed by any return you might receive from money that is not even yours to start with.

## STEALING THE TITLE DENOTES GREEDINESS

The wisdom of the Proverbs speaks to this point:

*A man with an evil eye hastens after riches, and does not consider that poverty will come upon him.*

Proverbs 28:22

The King James translation says it a little differently:

*He that hasteth to be rich hath an evil eye, and considereth not that poverty shall come upon him.*

Proverbs 28:22, KJV

Some people are consumed with the thought of getting rich. That's evil, the Bible shows us, and it's also dangerous. The end result is usually poverty, poverty of spirit and poverty of purse.

As I was meditating in preparation to preach this message for the first time, God spoke something to me that I had never heard before. He showed me that people within the Church, even in positions of leadership, have a serious gambling problem. How shocking! But this is a result of a lust for money, a desire to get rich quick. It will lead to destruction every time.

"Money," my mother always told me, "will burn a hole in your pocket." And it's true. There's something about money that is very corrupting. For every dollar that comes into our hands, we need to see only eighty cents that is ours to spend. Ten cents off of the top goes to God, another ten cents should go to savings, and the rest is ours to meet our current needs. But learn to manage your money well. Too many of us are poor money managers.

## TAKE YOUR TIME

And, on your way to prosperity, take your time. Don't rush it. There's no hurry. God will do it in His own time.

When a woman is pregnant and an ultrasound is taken, she can see the baby and gets excited about having it. But it's not time yet. That baby must remain in her for many more months and develop slowly, one day at a time. Eventually, although it seems like it will never come, the day of birth will arrive.

*God is assuring us*

It takes nine months, thirty-six weeks, and it can't be rushed. Even Jesus' preparation for ministry took Him more than thirty years. That's a long time, and His ministry itself only lasted three years. That was thirty years of preparation and three years of demonstration. So don't get in a hurry for prosperity. Let God do it in His own time and His own way.

*that there should be*

*no lack among us...*

So many of us bring stress and difficulty to our own lives simply because we can't wait. We know that something is intended for us, and we just can't wait for it to come in God's way. We have to force the issue.

God is assuring us that there should be no lack among us, and in this hour, He wants us to fear, reverence, and honor Him and to know that His Word is true. Let Him do the miracle in His own time.

## HIDDEN ISSUES CONCERNING FINANCES

Some of us have secret internal issues regarding finances. No one else knows about it, but it's there.

Some weeks ago, I was meeting with a group of men with whom we have formed a book club. We meet regularly and read together some good books. One day I noticed that while we were reading, a particular man was just staring at me. He never looked at his book. Later, he confided in me that he had never learned to read.

To look at that man, a person in his mid-fifties, you would never have known this fact about him. He loves the Lord and is a faithful member of the church, but he has this secret that hinders his spiritual progress. He confided in me that he had been challenged and was going to go back to school and learn to read.

our inner secret may be far different from that—and far more serious. And it may be holding you back, keeping you from the greater things God has for your life.

We so readily attribute every problem in our lives to the enemy of our souls, and he does his fair share. But our destiny is in our own hands. We must willingly place ourselves on the journey to prosperity. You won't just wake up one day and suddenly find that you're debt free. It takes planning. It takes strategizing. It takes sacrificing.

We have our slogans, like "more in 2004," and they make it sound so easy, but you don't just get more. You have to make your way to more, and then more will make its way to you.

## KEYS TO PROSPERITY

After the Israelites had successfully crossed the Red Sea, defeated many enemies they faced, and pressed forward toward the Promised Land, Moses felt compelled to rehearse in their hearing all that God had done lest they be exalted and forget God. Part of this rehearsing included important keys to financial prosperity. He said:

> *"Beware that you do not forget the Lord your God by not keeping His commandments, His judgments, and His statutes which I command you today, lest—when you have eaten and are full, and have built beautiful houses and dwell in them; and when your herds and your flocks multiply, and your silver and your gold are multiplied, and all that you have is multiplied; when your heart is lifted up, and you forget the Lord your God who brought you out of the land of Egypt, from the house of bondage; who led you through that great and terrible wilderness, in which were fiery serpents and scorpions and thirsty land where there was no water; who brought water for you out of the flinty rock; who fed you in the wilderness with manna, which your fathers did not know, that He might humble you and that He might test you, to do you good in the end—then you say in your heart, 'My power and the might of my hand have gained me this wealth.'*
>
> *"And you shall remember the Lord your God, for it is He who gives you power to get wealth, that He may establish His covenant which He swore to your fathers, as it is this day."*

Deuteronomy 8:11-18

The tithe is one of the ways that we prevent the tendency to forget God and to begin to think that we've done something to cause our own prosperity. The fact that we're called upon to tithe does not indicate that God needs anything from us. His kingdom is not short on cash. His kingdom lacks nothing.

Does God need my dime? Oh no! He wants me to tithe, not so that He can get my money, but so that His glory can be revealed in my life, so that others can see my prosperity and believe in Him.

"How are you doing so well with all of the financial challenges you have faced?" some may ask us, and that will be our opportunity to tell them about the goodness of our God. Others, who work the same job as you, may ask you how you remain so stress-free on the limited salary you make." That, again, will be your opportunity to let them know your secrets.

With all that God has done for you, whatever you do, don't forget Him. You prayed for that job, and He gave it to you. Don't ever forget it.

You asked God to make a way where there seemed to be no way, and He did. Now don't you forget it. He remembered you, so don't you forget Him.

## THE POWER TO GET WEALTH

God will give you the power (the right, the privilege and the authority) to get wealth. And why would He give you power to get something He didn't want you to have in the first place? This fact alone proves that He wants you to prosper.

In this life, you will deal with many challenges, but when you're serving God, money should not be one of those challenges. You have too many other things to deal with to have to believe God for a light bill to be paid. You're God's child, and He wants you to have more than just enough to get by with.

If you're doing wrong and walking contrary to God's commandments, then you can expect trouble. After all, you're under a curse. Everything will go wrong in your life. Your relationships will be under attack. Your children will be disobedient. And your health will suffer.

God can't lift that curse. You have to lift it yourself. You brought it on yourself, so now you need to remove it by living "right." Return to God, and He will return to you.

I've never been one to check the rolls of our church to see who's tithing and who's not, but believe me, God knows. And even though I may not know it by having looked at the financial record books, the life of each person reflects what they do or don't do. If a person is suffering from high blood pressure, and they're constantly worried, it may be because they're not being obedient to God in the tithe.

## IT'S TIME FOR CHANGE

It's time to be tired of the whole "mess" of your financial life and to cast the whole burden on God. In Jacob's prayer, he asked God to do certain things for him, and, in return, he promised God that he would tithe. You can do that too. Tell God, "Make my house a house of peace. Keep food on my table. Keep us all well clothed." But then don't you forget your part of the bargain. God keeps His promises to you, so you need to keep your promises to Him.

Get this matter of stewardship "right" with God today. Do better, and you will receive better. The tithe is not for God; it's for us.

Believe God today for supernatural favor upon your life, an anointing of prosperity. You may find that you're at the darkest hour of your life, but always remember that just before the breaking of day comes the darkest part of the night. Thank God for the breakthrough that's just on the horizon for you as you learn to obey Him in "right" stewardship of all that He has placed within your life.

With this, you will have taken one more positive step toward *Doing "Right" in a Wrong World.*

# CHAPTER 13

# "Right" Living Demands the "Right" Kind of Faith

*So Jesus came again to Cana of Galilee where He had made the water wine. And there was a certain nobleman whose son was sick at Capernaum. When he heard that Jesus had come out of Judea into Galilee, he went to Him and implored [begged or beseeched] Him to come down and heal his son, for he was at the point of death.*

*Then Jesus said to him, "Unless you people see signs and wonders, you will by no means believe."*

*The nobleman said to him, "Sir, come down before my child dies!"*

*Jesus said to him, "Go your way; your son lives."*

*So the man believed the word that Jesus spoke to him, and he went his way. And as he was now going down, his servants met him, and told him, saying, "Your son lives!"*

*Then he inquired of them the hour when he got better. And they said to him, "Yesterday at the seventh hour the fever left him."*

*So the father knew that it was the same hour in which Jesus had said to him, "Your son lives." And he himself believed, and his whole household.*

*This again is the second sign that Jesus did, when He had come out of Judea into Galilee.*

John 4:46-54

In this present season, many of us find our faith on trial, and the result is that we are lacking strong faith. Your faith is not what you know about God, but rather what you believe about Him. And you need it to be strong.

If you're feeling weak in faith today, lay hands on yourself right now and pray, "God, increase my faith." He wants to take you to a greater level of faith today.

In this story from John 4, Jesus had an encounter with faith. The man in the story was a nobleman, meaning that he was no Johnny Come Lately. He was known and respected in the community, and he had power, wealth, and prestige. This man had other people working for him, but, at the same time, he had a problem he could not resolve on his own.

Regardless of who you are, how high you rise, or your status and income, there will come a season in your life when you'll come up against situations that you cannot handle alone. Although the man had many resources at his disposal, when his son became desperately ill, he didn't know what to do about it. The child was so sick, in fact, that he was described as being *"at the point of death."*

Fortunately, this nobleman heard about Jesus and His power, and so he went and found the Lord and begged Him to come to his house and help him. The exchange of words between them teaches us many things about faith. For this particular chapter, we want to look at three obstacles to strong faith.

## VICARIOUS FAITH

The first obstacle to strong faith is something I call vicarious faith. According to *Miriam-Webster's Dictionary* this word *vicarious* means "experienced or realized through imaginative or sympathetic participation in the experience of another." I would define it simply as something secondhand, diluted, watered down, or passed down from another person. When you experience something vicariously, you're living it through someone else, not for yourself. This kind of faith will always serve as an obstacle to keep us from where we're ultimately supposed to be.

This nobleman came from Capernaum to Cana of Galilee because he heard that Jesus had done a great miracle there, turning water into wine. He didn't know Jesus himself; he had just heard about Him from someone else. On the basis of their report, he went seeking Jesus. If He had been able to turn water into wine and change the outcome of a wedding reception, then surely He could help him too.

But the nobleman could not get to heaven on someone else's faith, and you can't either. You can't go on my faith, your grandmother's faith, or the faith of a fellow church member. You can't even get to heaven on your prayer partner's faith. Each of us must have a personal, individual, and genuine faith in God for ourselves.

The reason some people cannot see a move of God within their life is that they're trying to relate to God through someone else's faith. It's time that they asked themselves this question: Do I just know *about* Jesus, or do I really know Him? Just because you know *about* Jesus doesn't mean that the power He possesses can become yours. In order for that power to pass from Him to you, you have to know Him for yourself.

You can't just have religion; you must have a relationship. You have to know that God has done things in your life that nobody else could take credit for. You must be able to testify, "I know that if it had not been for the Lord Who was on my side, things would have been very different for me." Most important of all, you must be able to say, "I know that I know Him."

This doesn't mean that you necessarily know everything you need to know about the Lord, but you know that you know Him. That's the foundation. That's where it all begins. And when you know Jesus, you also know that He'll make a way for you where there seems to be no way. You know that He'll supply your every need, and you know that He'll heal you when you're sick.

Do you know Him? The nobleman didn't. His faith was vicarious, not personal. And that's always a problem.

You can't just do what you see someone else doing and expect it to work the same way for you. Do what you do as a believer out of your own experience and reverence for God. What He's doing in someone else's life has nothing to do with what He wants to do in your life. He's done many things for others, but now you need Him to do some things for you.

What this nobleman was going through with his son was just a test of his faith. God wanted to draw him to Himself, so He allowed a circumstance to come to him that he couldn't handle and required that He seek the Lord.

God allows many situations to come to our lives so that we can come to know Him or come to know Him better. And that may be the reason our circumstances are sometimes so desperate. When desperation comes, only God can help us, and if He doesn't do something for us, nothing will change.

When these seemingly terrible things happen, relax. God has us right where He wants us. He doesn't want us to be able later to give someone else the credit for our deliverance. He is drawing us to Himself, and He is about to do a miracle for us. But that miracle cannot come about through vicarious faith. Get to know the Lord for yourself.

## A SIGN-DEMANDING FAITH

Another obstacle to strong faith is what I call a sign-demanding faith. When the nobleman told Jesus that his son was at home dying, Jesus' answer was this: *"Unless you people see signs and wonders, you will by no means believe"* (John 4:48). What does that mean?

Some people can't see God because they're trying to see Him in some particular way. They can't trust God because they want to see the result right now, and it doesn't always happen that way.

The Scriptures teach: *"The just shall live by faith"* (Romans 1:17, Galatians 3:11, and Hebrews 10:38). You have to come to the point that you're willing to say, "God, I just trust You. I can't go by what I see or by what I hear. If I pay attention to what I see and what I hear, it will surely hinder me." You must get to the point that you begin to call those things which be not as though they were (see Romans 4:17). Get your eyes off of what you see in the natural, and begin to see in the Spirit. Then you can say, "It's already done!"

When Jesus answered in this way, it almost sounded as if He was not feeling any concern at all for the man's son. Rather than immediately address the issue of the sick son, He chose to rebuke the nobleman for his misplaced faith. But since faith is everything, we have to get it "right."

I am sad to say that there exists right now in the evangelical body of believers a group of individuals who are looking for a miracle a minute, and when a real miracle doesn't show up, they fabricate a circumstance to make it seem like a miracle. But we don't have to go looking for miracles or signs. In fact, the Bible shows us that signs should be following us (see Mark 16:17). We should believe in miracles, but trust in Jesus. Never trust in miracles.

I'm not happy with all the talk among Christian circles today about miracles that are not rooted in the Word of God. This is dangerous for two reasons: (1) Because we are living in a time of New Age mysticism, and (2) Because the Bible says that *"a wicked and adulterous generation seeks after a sign"* (Matthew 16:4).

We all know that it's a sin to attribute to Satan the works of the Holy Spirit, but it's equally a sin to attribute to the Holy Spirit the works of Satan. I believe in miracles, but I also know what a miracle is and what a miracle isn't.

The attitude of some is: "Show me some proof!" and it's offensive to God. In essence, we're saying, "God, I have your Word, but that's not enough." That's like a slap in God's face. The person who speaks in this way dares to insult the Almighty.

If I were to suggest to my son that I wanted to place a hundred dollars a month into a special account set up for him so that when he was ready for college, there would be some money available for his studies, and he asked to see the deposit slips to be sure that I was keeping my promise, I would, quite naturally, be offended. Well, that's exactly how God feels when we questions His word.

"I know what You're saying, God, but just give me a sign. Show me some proof." That's offensive. It means that we can't take God at His word.

God is looking for children who will just take Him at His word. When He speaks of doing a certain thing, they will shout as if it's already done—knowing that when He speaks it, it *is* as good as done. They will go ahead and give Him glory while waiting for the sure manifestation of what He has spoken.

Praise God for what you know is already done and stop looking at what you see in the natural. If He made a promise and said it was done, then it's done.

Too many people are saying to God, "Give me a miracle that I can see, and then I'll believe." But faith works just the opposite way.

Many of the circumstances of life are designed so that God can intervene and we can see His handiwork, and this causes men to believe:

*Now when He was in Jerusalem at the Passover, during the feast, many believed in His name when they saw the signs which He did.*

John 2:23

But these people didn't believe in His name until they had seen the signs which He did. This didn't please the Lord:

*But Jesus did not commit Himself to them, because He knew all men.*

John 2:24

Isn't that interesting! They believed, and yet He didn't commit Himself to them. Why was that?

It is noteworthy that in the original Greek, the word here translated *believe* and the word translated *commit* are from the very same Greek word. They believed in Him, but He didn't believe in them. They believed in Him, but He didn't commit Himself to them.

Why? Because He sensed that they were only believing in Him for what He was able to do and for what they were able to see. They were not hungry for God; they were only hungry for signs. They wanted miracles, but they didn't want the God of miracles.

This kind of faith dishonors God. The proof is that although they believed in Him, He refused to commit Himself to them. The moment the signs stopped, He knew they would be gone. They were not seeking truth, and that's always a problem.

Far too many Christians are only serving God for what they can get from Him. They are willing to praise and worship God (as long as they can expect a Mercedes in return). They're willing to hear His Word (as long as it promises them a spouse or a promotion on their job). But, as true believers, we are to worship and serve God, not because of what we can get from Him, but because of who He is to us. He is our everything, our all in all, and when we place our focus on Him, then everything else will come.

It's not right to come to God just for "stuff." If you do that, in the moment the "stuff" stops flowing, you'll turn your back on Him. If you lost absolutely everything, would you still serve God? That's the test of true faith.

Too many people, when the road gets a little rocky or when some persecution begins to arise against them, react by turning their backs on God. That's not the type of disciples He needs and wants.

If your brand-new car were to be totally demolished, would you still love God? If your house were to be inundated with water, would you still be praising Him?

Pastors and elders who lead Christian congregations everywhere need to have a spirit of discernment. Not everyone who attends a worship service or a Bible study is committed to the cause of Christ. Many of them may be only committed to what they think a congregation can do for them.

This is true for individuals as well. There are people who will work their way into your life and try to get close to you just so that they can get something from you. When you no longer have anything to give them, they'll walk away from you.

That was the nobleman's problem. He was not after Jesus. He was after signs. When the miracles stopped, would he still be serving God? Would he still be committed to Him?

Even some of those who accept a position in a local church are often not truly committed to the pastor of the church and his vision. They want something, and if they don't get it, they'll eventually walk away from that church. The minute someone is not paying them enough attention, they'll be gone. That's sign-demanding faith, and it's offensive to the Lord.

Thomas has often been called the doubting disciple. When some of the other disciples told him that they had seen Jesus alive after His crucifixion, He said to them:

*Unless I see in His hands the print of the nails, and put my finger into the print of the nails, and put my hand into His side, I will not believe.*

John 20:25

Eight days later, Jesus appeared to the disciples again, and this time Thomas was present. The Lord turned to Thomas and spoke to him directly:

*Then He said to Thomas, "Reach your finger here, and look at My hands; and reach your hand here, and put it into My side. Do not be unbelieving, but believing."*

John 20:27

The response of Thomas was heartening. He exclaimed: *"My Lord and my God!"* (John 20:28). Then Jesus said to him:

*Thomas, because you have seen Me, you have believed. Blessed are those who have not seen and yet have believed.*

John 20:29

That's real faith, believing without having to see.

There has to come a time in your life when you commit yourself to an uncompromising position in God. If He doesn't move, you will not move either. You're determined to stand upon His Word. This may cause you to look rather silly to other members of your family and to your friends, but you don't care about that. You'll stand anyway.

*When you're fully persuaded that what He has promised He will do, nothing and no one can move you.*

God has spoken, and you know that He'll keep His Word. So that's the end of the discussion.

When you take such a stand, God will eventually make a way for you because you have declared it to everyone around you. God's name is on the line, so He has to move. His reputation is at stake. He cannot fail or He would no longer be God.

When you're fully persuaded that what He has promised He will do, nothing and no one can move you. You can stand on His Word without wavering.

Thomas had believed because he had seen, but Jesus said that the most blessed ones would be those who had not yet seen, but had believed anyway. You can start praising God on credit for what you haven't yet seen, for it will surely come to pass. Praise God now, and He will bless you later.

There's an old saying, "Seeing is believing," but that's not true. Seeing is seeing, and believing is believing. And you don't need the one to have the other.

"If you show it to me, then I'll believe it" is the attitude of many. In their case, the saying is true. Seeing *is* believing. But that's not how we Christians are to live. If you already see something, then you no longer need to believe for it. You already have it. Believing is for things you can't yet see.

Because you can't see a thing, you must believe. Once you can see it, then you can stop believing. Don't be guilty of demanding a sign from God. Believe, and see His mighty hand at work.

Jesus came to earth to save souls, not to perform miracles. He did perform miracles, but that was not His purpose in coming. This lets us know that we must go beyond miracles and make it to Jesus. Believe in miracles, but trust in the Miracle Worker.

## SELF-CENTERED FAITH

A third deadly type of faith that prevents the blessings of God from flowing in the lives of many is what I call self-centered faith. This nobleman had only heard of Jesus, and when he met Him and asked for His help, Jesus said to him: *"Unless you people see signs and wonders, you will by no means believe,"* (John 4:48). The nobleman's answer was rather strange, *"Sir, come down before my child dies"* (John 4:49). He didn't really answer Jesus' charge. All he could think about was his own need, his son, who was even then at death's door.

He hadn't bothered to bow at the feet of Jesus, or to worship and honor Him in any way. He had a one-track mind, and all he knew to do was to tell Jesus what he wanted. Was this any way to approach the Son of God?

The first words out of the man's mouth were not words of praise for Jesus, but *"my child."* This was a selfish and self-centered faith. The nobleman had no time to recognize and honor Jesus, only to ask for His help.

The woman with the issue of blood knew what to do. She fell at Jesus' feet and began to worship Him (see Luke 8:37). His response to her was far different than it was to the nobleman.

There's nothing wrong with asking God to help you. You need to do that. But there is a way to ask. It's not a demanding way. It's not a selfish way. It's a loving, trusting way.

*"Come down before my child dies,"* the nobleman said. But Jesus refused to acquiesce to this request.

"No," He said, "you go."

We're asking God to come, and He wants us to go.

"Come, Jesus," he insisted.

"No," the Master answered. "You go."

True faith is not necessarily receiving from God exactly what you want. It may be accepting from God what He allows. God may not give you exactly what you want simply because He knows what's best for you. He may not always give you what you want, but He'll always give you what you need.

For instance, you may have been wanting to leave your job, but if God is keeping you there, it must be for a reason. Don't leave before it's time to leave.

## CHANGED FAITH

If the nobleman in this story was so dependant on the faith of others, so demanding, and so selfish, why is his story even in the Bible? Does his story deserve to be told? It's there because something changed, and that change is reflected in verse 50: *"So the man believed the word that Jesus spoke to him, and he went his way."* When this man believed, he suddenly dropped his defensiveness and began to obey Jesus.

God has given each of us eyes that respond to light and ears that respond to sound, but He also created us with a spirit that was intended to respond to the character and the nature of God. Real faith is characterized by obedience. It is impossible to believe God and trust Him and still not obey Him. That's not real faith.

This may well be the faith the Bible speaks of as being *"dead"* (James 2:20 and 26). But now the nobleman had an alive and vibrant faith, and it produced the desired result. As he was nearing his home, his servants met him with the good news: *"Your son lives!"* (John 4:51). They hadn't expected him to live, and the nobleman had wondered if he would ever see his son alive again, but true faith changed all that.

Faith that does not lead to obedience is not faith at all. True faith is not doing what you want to do. It's not trusting God when it's convenient. True faith comes into play when you don't feel like doing something God has said, but you do it anyway. True faith comes into play when you cannot yet see what God has promised, but you obey Him anyway. True faith comes into play when you can't yet understand what God has said, but you obey Him nevertheless.

As we noted, the nobleman was from Capernaum. He had gone to Cana, a distance of some twenty miles or more, to seek Jesus. In those days, travel was extremely slow and laborious, and he evidently had other things to do. By the time he got home again, it was already the next day.

When they told him that his son had recovered, he asked them when the change had occurred. Their answer was: *"Yesterday at the seventh hour the fever left him"* (John 4:52). The nobleman knew that this was the very same moment in which Jesus had spoken the words, *"Your son lives."* And, as if to emphasize that fact, the servants had greeted him with those very words.

What you're believing God for is happening right now, and you, too, can expect to see the results of your faith very soon. You asked God for it, and He sent His Word to perform it. At this moment, it's happening.

That change you've been needing on your job is happening. That change you've been asking God for in your finances is happening. Rejoice in it.

Suddenly this nobleman got very excited. Jesus had not moved from His spot in Cana, and yet the miracle had taken place. Jesus had not needed to travel to Capernaum. He had simply spoken the word, and it happened. He had been some twenty miles away, and had not seen or physically touched the sick child, and yet the child was healed. Distance is clearly no problem for our God. He's the master of all time and space.

## FAITH AND MORE FAITH

Now, as this all dawned on the nobleman, a great change began to come over him. The others might not have known and understood exactly what had happened, but he did.

Jesus had not prayed a prayer or spoken a blessing. He had simply said, *"Your son lives,"* but that had been enough. In that very moment, it happened. The power of the sickness had been broken, and his son had been healed.

The next words the Bible records are telling: *"And he himself believed"* (John 4:53). The nobleman had believed in verse 50, but now he was really believing. And his newfound faith was contagious. Not only did he believe, but because he believed, *"his whole household"* also believed.

And this newfound faith had a wonderful dimension. This family was not just believing in miracles. They were believing in the Miracle Worker.

173

The lateness of the nobleman's arrival at home is also a demonstration of his faith. It was now more than twenty-four hours after he had met Jesus. He had gone to the Lord with one thing and only one thing on his mind, and you would think that after Jesus spoke those words, *"Your son lives,"* the man would have rushed home to see if it was true. As I noted earlier, apparently he had other matters to attend to, and besides, if Jesus said it was done, then it was done.

So what are we so worried about? And why should we worry about anything? We pray about certain situations and feel that we've turned them over to God, and yet we continue to carry the burden of them. The result is that we're "all stressed out" over situations that are already on their way to resolution.

When you've prayed about something, and it only seems to get worse, don't give up. That's the time to really believe God, to really trust Him. If you've committed it to Him, then He has done it. Thank Him and rest in His provision.

And if you need a right-now miracle, our God is a right-now God. Believe Him, trust Him, and then worship Him until your situation gets better. Nothing is impossible with God if we can only believe.

## WHO DO YOU TRUST?

We're very strange about who we do and do not trust. For instance, we go into a pharmacy, where we don't know anyone at all, hand the pharmacist a prescription that we often can't read, and trust him to fill it correctly. We don't even know for sure if he has gone to pharmaceutical school.

He gives us some pills, and we don't know what color their supposed to be or if they're made up of the right compounds. But, because the instructions on the bottle are to take two of them with a glass of water, we do it without question.

Think about that for a moment. You couldn't decipher the prescription, you don't know for sure that your doctor has gone to an accredited medical school, and you don't know for sure if your pharmacist is a real pharmacist, and yet you take the medicine believing that it will help you. That's faith, but might it be misguided?

You don't know. Your regular pharmacist could be tied up in the back of the drug store, and the person filling your prescription could be someone who knows nothing about pharmacy, but has only donned a pharmacist's jacket. Still, you take the pills and trust them to help you get better.

If you can trust a person you don't even know in this way, how can you not trust God? He was with your grandmother and then your mother, and now He's with you. And He has not changed. Trust Him. Praise Him now for the answer to your prayers. The work is done.

This done, you're making amazing progress toward *Doing "Right" in a Wrong World.*

# CHAPTER 14

# Doing the "Right" Thing
# When You Don't Want to Do It

*Then Jesus came with them to a place called Gethsemane, and said to the disciples, "Sit here while I go and pray over there." And He took with him Peter and the two sons of Zebedee, and He began to be sorrowful and deeply distressed.*

*Then He said to them, "My soul is exceedingly sorrowful, even to death. Stay here and watch with Me."*

*He went a little farther and fell on His face, and He prayed, saying, "O My Father, if it is possible, let this cup pass from Me; nevertheless, not as I will, but as You will."*

Matthew 26:36-39

The message of this final chapter of the book will send your life into a new spiritual dimension if you're willing to heed it. It will take you into that which God has purposed, ordained, and destined for your life from ages past. This word is so timely and so pregnant with truth that just reading the scriptures contained in it could spark new birth in you today. And all of this will help you to start *Doing the "Right" Thing.*

As I've been emphasizing throughout the book, we're called not just to do some "good" thing, but to do the "right" thing, the thing that's pleasing to God, the thing that He has destined us for from the foundation of the world. Doing the "right" thing, living "right," is not the norm today in our modern world, and it can be extremely challenging. But the only safe life is the "right" life, because when you're doing what's "right," you're guaranteed safety and success. When you're doing what's "right," you don't even have to worry about your enemies. God will take care of every one of them.

## WHEN DOING THE "RIGHT" THING IS NOT CONVENIENT

But when living "right" and doing the "right" thing, there are times when we have to do what we don't want to do. This was even true for Jesus, and He's in a category all by Himself.

Jesus' short years on earth made such an impact on every succeeding period of history that unbelievers struggle to explain it. While not wanting to concede that He was God, they find it difficult to explain the lasting impact He made any other way. In the end, they conclude that maybe He didn't exist at all. Maybe He was just a figment of men's imaginations, a mythological figure.

But Jesus not only lived and walked on this earth; He is even now alive and seated at the right hand of the Father making intercession for you and me. He was God then, and He's God now. Still, He had to do something He didn't want to do.

When Jesus came to earth, He did so as wholly God and wholly man. He was at the same time both God and man. Usually, both God and man in Him were at peace with one another. In this case, however, His deity and His humanity collided. His man side cringed at the thought of taking upon Himself not only the sins of all mankind, but also the results of sin, the wages of sin, the suffering caused by sin. At the same time, the God side of Him knew that He must.

The point is: if Jesus had to do something that He didn't want to do, how much more will this be true of us? It would be wonderful to always choose the easy path in life, to avoid the difficult decisions and the demanding challenges. But those of us who make a choice to live "right" and do "right" also choose to face some of life's hardships—whether we like it or not.

For instance, Paul wrote to Timothy, his son in the faith:

*Yes, and all who desire to live godly in Christ Jesus will suffer persecution.*

2 Timothy 3:12

Who will suffer? *"All who desire to live godly in Christ Jesus."* We don't want to suffer, and we'll do almost anything to avoid suffering. Yet, if we want to live "right," we will suffer.

True Christians, just because they are true Christians, will be called on to endure certain snubs and slights, and even physical and verbal abuse. They will endure these things on their jobs, in the communities where they live, and even sometimes in their own home.

I wish it was not true, but it is. I wish I could tell you that there was some way you could fulfill the will of God in your life without having to suffer any wrong, but it's simply not so.

Paul wrote to the Philippian believers:

*For to you it has been granted on behalf of Christ, not only to believe in Him, but also to suffer for His sake.*

Philippians 1:29

Our suffering for Christ's sake can take other forms. For instance, God gives us goals, dreams, objectives, and visions, but in order to see these realized, we must make some sacrifice, undergo some type of deprivation, give something up, surrender something to God and His will.

## ANY WORTHY GOAL REQUIRES SACRIFICE

This is also true of those who work toward any worthy goal in the world. An athlete, for instance, is sometimes able to sign a multimillion-dollar contract and to gain instantaneous popularity, but in order to do that, he first has to subject himself to a rigorous training regime. There are certain foods that he simply cannot eat and others that he must eat whether he likes it or not. He must subject his body to hours of painful and, at times, torturous daily preparation.

There are also curfews that must be obeyed and practice times that must be honored, and endless hours in the gym that are essential if any athlete is to stay in tip-top shape. If any athlete decides that it's not worth the effort and begins to slack off, some other athlete is waiting to take his place.

Professional athletes spend a lot of time on the road away from their families, and because they often get traded, they must be ready at any time to pack up their families and move to another city, sometimes a city they don't even like. This inconveniences the entire family, as children are taken out of school and have to find new schools and new friends in a strange place.

Businessmen who want to become entrepreneurs and start their own businesses should know ahead of time what they're getting themselves into. For one thing, they're risking their own capital, their life's savings, or perhaps their inheritance. True, the business may have their name on the door, but there's a heavy price tag attached to it. Many new businesses fail, and that entrepreneur may lose everything. Is he willing to start all over again if that happens?

Business owners must be willing to put in some very long hours to make their businesses work. Theirs is never a nine-to-five existence. When any employee doesn't show up, the owners have to do the work. They have no choice. And until faithful employees can be found and trained, like it or not, the owners will keep doing the work. There are rewards, but there are also trade-offs.

A parent who has been blessed with a beautiful child usually cannot think of any negatives involved with the birth of that child into the family, but those negatives won't take long in coming. And there are many of them. For instance, when a baby comes along, suddenly your independence is greatly limited, if not entirely eliminated. If you want to go anywhere at all, you either have to lug the baby along with you, or you have to get a babysitter. The result is that you don't go many of the places you would like to go. You give that up for the sake of your child.

When that child begins to cry in the wee hours of the morning, and you don't feel like getting up, you suddenly realize that there's no one else to do it. You're the parent, and that's your responsibility. You're tired, and you need your rest, but you have no choice but to get up and attend to the child.

Jobs are also demanding. If you can land a good one, you're very happy about that. The idea of doing something you like to do or of having the stable income such a job affords is pleasing. You rejoice. Right now you're not thinking about the fact that fully one third of your waking hours will be given to that company. You will not be your own person, but will be told what to do from day to day. You may not like the environment in which you have to work or the people you have to work for and with. And you will have little control over your future, for you are now at the mercy of your employer. This will all dawn on you in time, and then you'll wonder if you've made the right choice in accepting the job after all.

There are always trade-offs in life. In order to gain something, you have to give something. The young man or woman who decides to go on a diet looks forward to a more pleasing appearance, to getting into smaller clothes, or even of landing a suitable mate. For the moment, they're not considering the deprivation they will suffer from giving up their favorite foods and denying themselves extra helpings when they still feel hungry. They're only thinking of the objective to be reached. The high price of weight loss will dawn on them very quickly, and they'll realize what they have to pay for what they want out of life.

I know this is not something we like to hear, but we must hear it. Everything in life has its price, and if we want to be our best, we'll have to do some things we don't really want to do.

This message is particularly difficult for our younger generations. They've grown up having their every whim met, and they're not accustomed to disappointment of any kind. "If it feels good, do it," has been their guiding counsel in life. But that has to change and quickly, or they're in for some rude surprises. Life involves many sacrifices, and some of them seem too great to bear.

## JESUS HAD A LOT TO LOSE

Jesus was having a good time in life. He was only thirty-three, He had made a lot of friends, and His ministry was being widely accepted and appreciated. He was doing a lot of good, and He didn't want to die just then.

Secondly, the thought of somehow bearing the sins of all mankind suddenly became overwhelming. The wages of sin are dreadful, and Jesus would be called upon to suffer the wages of sin, not just for one man, but for all men of all times in all places—past, present, and future. Could He even bear up under it? He wasn't sure that He could.

But, most of all, Jesus did not want to be separated from His Father, and drinking the cup that was being offered to Him required it.

He had never been separated from His Father. They had created the worlds together, and the thought of such a separation was too painful for contemplation.

To the man side of Jesus, the thought of all of this was absolutely revolting. He couldn't bear it, and He turned away in disgust. But the God side of Him knew that there was no other way. This was why He had come to the earth in the first place, and He simply had to do it—like it or not. These two sides of Him now collided head-on.

Jesus the man now pleaded with the Father to find some other way, any other way, to save mankind. He knew that He had been sent to earth to do it, but could it not be accomplished in some other, more reasonable, way? This was just too much to bear.

The Garden of Gethsemane where Jesus prayed this prayer was not so far from Golgotha, where He was to die. Some have imagined that He saw Himself there and what He would suffer. If so, He could see Himself being nailed to the cross, see His side being pierced by a spear, see the crown of thorns being thrust upon His head.

In all of this, He would experience excruciating pain. Could He bear it? He wasn't sure that He could, and His humanity cried out to God for some other way. *"If it be possible,"* He prayed, *"let this cup pass from me."*

Only one who had experienced it could know the agony behind those words. And Jesus was now in such agony of prayer that His sweat came as great drops of blood.

"Is there no other way?" He cried. "Can the same thing not be accomplished some other way? Must I drink this bitter cup, this cup of suffering, this cup of pain, this cup of death? Is there no other way?"

At this point, Jesus paused. In the biblical text, this is not apparent. It goes from one phrase into the next. But the two phrases were, in essence, spoken by two very different people. The first phrase was spoken by the man Jesus, and then the God in Him took over and spoke the second phrase: *"Nevertheless not as I will, but as You will."*

Yes, this was the right course. It was not pleasant. In fact, it seemed unbearable for any man. Yet, Jesus knew that He could do it. He could do anything. To His flesh, it was revolting and disturbing, but He knew that it was "right," and He came to do what was "right" and to set for us a standard of rightness or righteousness.

He didn't want to go to the cross, but He knew that He had to do it. He didn't want to drink the cup, but He knew that He had to do it. He didn't want to be separated from the Father, but He knew that He had to be. If He didn't do it, the Father's will for His life could never be realized, and all of mankind would be forever lost.

Today many of us are spiritually where Jesus was physically in the Garden of Gethsemane. We may not be crucified, and we may not have to suffer sin for all mankind, but we will be called upon to do things that we utterly loathe.

## THE MAN JESUS NEEDED THE PRAYERS OF OTHERS

When Jesus went into Gethsemane that night, He took His disciples with Him. All of them were there except Judas, who had already set in motion his murderous plot. Jesus told them to sit and pray for Him while He went ahead for something He had to do alone.

Gethsemane was an olive garden that sat at the base of the Mount of Olives just across the Kidron Valley from Jerusalem. The name Gethsemane meant olive press, and so this was the place of crushing.

Olive products were one of the most sought-after commodities of Jesus' day. Aside from its obvious cooking uses, many things were made from the olive oil—including perfumes, medicines, and embalming fluid. But in order to get the oil, the olives had to be crushed. Jesus, too, had to be crushed. And, as much as we hate to hear it, each of us must be willing to be crushed—if God is to bring forth from our lives the very best that He desires.

It's time that someone told us that before we can begin to live our dreams, before our vision comes to pass, before we can step over into our God-ordained purpose, before we can apprehend our destiny, we, too, must go through the Garden of Gethsemane.

In the garden, the place of crushing, the outer is broken, so that the inner can be released. If all hell seems to be breaking loose in your life, and you feel under pressure as if you're being crushed, it's only because you are where Jesus was in Gethsemane. Before you panic and turn and run, consider this: Jesus was only moments away from His destiny, and you may be only moments away from greatness. Don't back down.

The things that come to your life are not just happenstance. Affliction may serve as a barometer to indicate that you're closer now than ever before to your purpose, your destiny, your goals, and your objectives being fulfilled. Rejoice in that and stand strong through every test.

*The things that come to your life are not just happenstance.*

Jesus was under severe pressure. He said: *"My soul is exceedingly sorrowful, even to death"* (verse 38). He somehow wished that His disciples could understand what He was going through, but they couldn't.

The pressure had become so intense that He wondered if He could bear it. When He used the words *"to death,"* He meant exactly that. It felt like He was nearing death.

Everything was happening at once. People were betraying Him. Beloved disciples were turning against Him. Angry men wanted Him dead. Even His disciples were falling asleep when He needed them the most. He had given them a new life, but now they were "too tired" to stay awake and help Him with their prayers in His greatest hour of need.

What Jesus was now experiencing was unprecedented and unheard of. The worst of it was the torment inside His mind and the agony of drinking the cup of sin and being cursed because of it. He had been called upon to be the sin-bearer for the whole world, and the agony of it was more than He could bear.

## THREE IMPORTANT STEPS TO VICTORY AND DESTINY

Three things that Jesus did brought Him victory, and if you will do those same three things, victory will come to your life as well. Let's look at it again:

> *He said to them, "My soul is exceedingly sorrowful even to death, stay here and watch with Me." He went a little farther, fell on His face, and prayed, saying, "O My Father, if it is possible, let this cup pass from Me; nevertheless, not as I will, but as You will."*
>
> Matthew 26:38-39

When the moment comes that you have to do what you don't want to do, the first thing to remember is to be honest with God. That's exactly what Jesus did. Our unwillingness to open up to God and tell the truth often holds us back. Talk to Him openly and honestly.

"God, I don't want to do this. You already know that. I can fool people, but I can never fool You. My flesh rebels against the very idea of fulfilling what You're saying to me. To my flesh, it's abhorrent, and my soul wants to cry out 'No'! Please help me. I'm weak, and if You don't help me now, I'm afraid that I'll fail. And I don't want to fail You again.

"In the past, You spoke to me some hard things, and I couldn't receive them. I failed You then, and I don't want to fail You again now. I'm determined to apprehend my destiny by doing what You've called me to do. But I need Your help now, or I will surely die."

If you cannot be honest with God and express your need to Him, you will never step over into your true purpose and destiny. Nothing will change. If you *can* be honest with God, He's there waiting to help you and give you His strength to carry you through each trial.

The second thing Jesus did was to submit His will to the Father. His flesh cried out, *"If it be possible, let this cup pass from Me,"* but then He knew what He had to do, and He prayed, *"Nevertheless, not as I will, but as You will"* (verse 39). Thus, He bowed to the will of the Father.

I have to admit that this is a difficult step, but I also have to insist that it's not impossible. You can submit your will to God—even in cases where you don't want to do it. In one sense, not submitting is childish and immature. After all, God is trying to do something wonderful in our lives, so why would we resist Him? He's trying to bring all of our greatest dreams to pass, so why should we stall and look for a way out?

Stop being so narrow minded. See things as God sees them. Look past the moment and into eternity. Once you get past this thing your flesh hates, what's on the other side will be glorious.

And can we not trust God? Did He not say:

*No temptation has overtaken you except such as is common to man; but God is faithful, who will not allow you to be tempted beyond what you are able, but with the temptation will also make the way of escape, that you may be able to bear it.*

1 Corinthians 10:13

God will never, NEVER place on you more than you can bear. He has promised it. So submit your will to His, and trust Him for your tomorrows.

Jesus looked to the disciples for comfort in this hour, but He found none. They had not prayed, as He asked them to, but had fallen asleep and forgotten about praying for Him:

*Then He came to the disciples and found them asleep, and said to Peter, "What, could you not watch with Me one hour? Watch and pray, lest you enter into temptation. The Spirit is indeed willing, but the flesh is weak."*

Matthew 26:40-41

Then He did it all a second time:

*He went away again, a second time and prayed, saying, "O My Father, if this cup cannot pass from Me unless I drink it, Your will be done."*

Matthew 26:42

That's the message of this chapter, and here's an important statement that you must digest: **When your will dies, your destiny lives!** Because we have not crucified our own will, the will of the flesh, we are needlessly holding up our destiny.

I served in the military, and before our company was shipped out to the front, we were all required to make and sign a will. This was something most of us African-Americans had never even thought of doing (and many African-Americans are still hesitant to do it today). But having a will is important.

A will is a legal document stating who has the right to any properties or goods that have belonged to us. It never hurts to make such a will because it can never be enforced until we're already dead. If we should die, and no will is found, there is often confusion and conflict among family members over what we really wanted done with our possessions in the event of death. So you need to make a will.

Then you need to find out if you are included in the wills of other family members. If something has been left to you, why not claim it?

Now, how does this apply to our subject? Well, Jesus died, but before He did, He left a will for us to read. Have you read it? Are you in it?

186

I'm not talking about being a member of the Church. I'm asking if you're in God's will? You may be able to sing beautifully, but are you in the will?

Although technically Jesus died His physical death at Calvary, the truth is that He had already died in Gethsemane. By the time He arrived at Calvary, He was already dead. His will died in the garden of pressing, and that's why He was able to checkmate the devil at Calvary. The devil was rejoicing, thinking that He was killing Jesus on Calvary, but Jesus had already willingly given His life for us in Gethsemane. And you can't kill a dead man. In the same way, if you can die to your own will, there's nothing the devil can do to you.

Third, when you have to do what you don't want to do, you must realize that even in suffering, you have God's presence with you. That makes all the difference.

You can pray, "Lord, I'm here because You have me here. What I'm experiencing is difficult and challenging. I've never been this way before, and my flesh wonders if I can bear it. But I have determined to get self out of the way. It is self that has been holding me back all along. And I know that You're with me in this moment."

This will frighten the devil. He'll take one look at you and know that you're a force to be reckoned with. He has long known that if you ever got your "self" out of the way, there would be no way of stopping you.

When Jesus went back to see how the disciples were doing, He was disappointed by what He found:

> *And He came and he found them asleep again, for their eyes were heavy. So He left them, went away again, and prayed the third time, saying the same words.*
>
> Matthew 26:43

The disciples had failed their Lord. They had fallen asleep again, when He had specifically asked them to stay awake and pray with Him. His response to this discovery was the following:

> *"Are you still sleeping and resting? Behold, the hour is at hand, and the Son of Man is being betrayed into the hands of sinners. Rise, let us be going. See, he who betrays Me is at hand."*
>
> Matthew 26:45-46

Jesus knew His fate, and He knew that His betrayer was at hand. He knew exactly what He was facing. He had known all along what Judas would do. He knew it the day He chose him. It was inevitable, and now was the time for its fulfillment.

He had finished His praying and His weeping, and it was now time for action. He had always been there for His disciples, but when He needed them the most, they were not available to Him. But He said nothing further about it. It was okay. They couldn't bear with Him, but God had not forsaken Him. And even through His darkest hour of suffering, the presence of the Father would sustain Him.

## JESUS' DARKEST HOUR

That, too, would change. Because of sin, because of God's hatred of sin, and because Jesus would actually become sin for us (see 2 Corinthians 5:21), He must now be separated from His Father. This breaking point would come as He was hanging on the cross for our sins. At that point, He suddenly cried out something that had not been heard before:

*And about the ninth hour Jesus cried out with a loud voice, saying, "Eli, Eli, lama sabachthani?" that is, "My God, My God, why have You forsaken Me?"*

Matthew 27:46

Does this make sense? Jesus was God, and yet He said that God was forsaking Him. Here, again we see His flesh, His humanity, clashing with His deity. He had known the plan of salvation before the worlds were formed, and yet in this moment, the man in Him felt the unbearable weight of it all, and He cried out to His Father.

Why would our loving heavenly Father forsake Jesus in His hour of need? Many doubt that the Father would actually have forsaken Jesus, but they're wrong. He *had* to forsake Jesus, for as Jesus hung there on the cross, He did so totally contaminated with every sin known to mankind. In that moment, Jesus was a child molester, a murderer, an extortionist, an alcoholic, a drug user, a rapist, a thief, and a liar. Every single one of your shortcomings and their awful consequences was attached to Him. And so were mine.

In that moment, Jesus had to bear in His body all sicknesses. He had AIDS as He hung on the cross of Calvary. He was eaten up with cancer, tuberculosis, and kidney disease. He must not only bear sin, but also the terrible results of sin.

God the Father had to turn His face from Jesus that day, but He did it so that He would never have to turn His back on you and me. Jesus was separated from the Father so that we could be united with the Father.

*Today, your victory is in your yes.*

Today, your victory is in your yes. Say to God right now, "God, I'm tired of fighting You and Your will for my life. Right now, I lay my will aside, and from this day forth, I will do things Your way, the "right" way. Doing only what is "good," what is acceptable to man, has kept back my blessings. Today, here in my Gethsemane, I yield all to You, knowing that You have my best interests at heart in all that You do. Your will be done in everything.

"I have now taken one step closer to my purpose, my dream, my objectives, and my goals. Thank You that even in our suffering You're with us."

## THE NINTH-HOUR ANOINTING

It all came to a climax at *"the ninth hour"*:

*Sitting down, they kept watch over Him there. And they put up over His head the accusation written against Him:*

*THIS IS JESUS*

*THE KING OF THE JEWS.*

*Then two robbers were crucified with Him, one on the right and another on the left. And those who passed by blasphemed Him, wagging their heads and saying, "You who destroy the temple and build it in three days, save Yourself! If You are the Son of God, come down from the cross."*

*Likewise the chief priests, also mocking with the scribes and elders said, "He saved others; Himself He cannot save. If He is the King of Israel, let Him now come down from the cross and we will believe Him. He trusted in God; let Him deliver Him now, if He will have Him; for He said, 'I am the Son of God.' "*

*Even the robbers who were crucified with Him reviled Him with the same thing.*

*Now from the sixth hour until the ninth hour there was darkness all over the land. And about the ninth hour Jesus cried with a loud voice....*

Matthew 27:36-45

Saints of God, it's the ninth month, the time for birthing. Your pain has suddenly intensified, and your contractions are coming closer together. It's time to alert everyone around you, to send out the alarm. The time has come. It's also the ninth hour, and God is giving you a ninth-hour anointing.

Luke recorded in the Acts of the Apostles:

*Now Peter and John went up together to the temple at the hour of prayer, the ninth hour. And a certain man lame from his mother's womb was carried, whom they laid daily at the gate of the temple which is called Beautiful, to ask alms from those who entered the temple; who, seeing Peter and John about to go into the temple, asked for alms. And fixing his eyes on him, with John, Peter said, "Look at us."*

*So he gave them his attention, expecting to receive from them. Then Peter said, "Silver and gold I do not have, but what I do have I give you: In the name of Jesus Christ of Nazareth, rise up and walk."*

Acts 3:1-6

It happened at the ninth hour.

*There was a certain man in Caesarea called Cornelius, a centurion of what was called the Italian Regiment, a devout man, and one who feared God with all of his household, who gave alms generously to the people, and prayed to God always. About the ninth hour of the day he saw clearly in a vision an angel of God coming in and saying to him, "Cornelius!"*

Acts 10:1-3

It happened at the ninth hour. And now it's your time, and your victory is in your yes.

The lame man at the Beautiful Gate was healed at the ninth hour, Cornelius saw the heavens opened at the ninth hour, and you need your ninth-hour blessing today. God will send His mighty power to make you whole, and He will cause the heavens to open for you.

Cornelius was said to be a good man, a generous giver, and a man of prayer. In the ninth hour, his prayers were answered, his goodness was recognized, and his generosity was rewarded.

And now it's your time for blessing too. Armed with all of the truths I have presented in this book, you're ready to begin *Doing "Right" in a Wrong World.*